Disasters

John Walker

DISASTERS

𝒇 Follett Publishing Company/Chicago

© John Walker 1973
Published in the United States
by Follett Publishing Company: 1973
First published in Great Britain
by Studio Vista Publishers: 1973

Filmset in 11 point Ehrhardt and printed by
BAS Printers Limited, Wallop, Hampshire

All rights reserved. No part of this publication may be
reproduced, stored in a retrieval system, or transmitted,
in any form or by any means, electronic, mechanical,
photocopying, recording, or otherwise, without the prior
written permission of the publisher.

ISBN 0-695-80399-9

Library of Congress Catalog Card Number: 72-96871

Contents

Prologue 6

1 The uneasy balance: man and his environment 10

2 Appointments in Samarra: travelling to death 34

3 All fall down: bridge and dam disasters 85

4 A captive audience: sporting and entertainment disasters 99

5 The way the world ends: explosion and fire 113

6 Suffer the little children 135

Epilogue: Woodstock and Altamont—the future? 144

Bibliography 150

Index 151

Prologue

A dictionary will define a disaster as a calamity, a sudden or great misfortune. Here, I have narrowed down that definition, excluding for the most part natural disasters, at least to the extent that they are outside our control. Instead I have concentrated on disasters that were avoidable, less acts of God than acts of man, or those where the consequences of an act of God were greatly worsened by the acts or omissions of man.

Such catastrophes bring out the best and the worst in those involved. The best is evident in the unselfish help, of money, time, even lives, that people are prepared to offer to aid the unfortunate. If that aspect seems occasionally overlooked in the accounts that follow, it is because it is the worst aspects of human nature that need emphasizing, for they can be changed. Most disasters should never happen. They are caused by indolence, apathy, greed, complacency, cowardice, ignorance. If we are not all capable of heroism, we can at least attempt to act with consideration for others.

A disaster is an accident on a large scale, and accidents happen all the time. Their ubiquity is astounding, if often small enough to pass unremarked. One of the reasons road deaths cause so little impact is that they happen little by little.

Take, as an example of the never-ending succession of accidents, mostly avoidable, the first few days of a recent month:

Thursday A jet is slightly damaged at Orly airport, France, after its nose-wheel ploughs into soft earth during fog. A driverless electric locomotive runs away at Harrogate, England, for ten miles, smashing two level-crossing gates. Three people die at Ingolstadt, Bavaria, after two trains carrying oil crash and explode in flames. Later, the railway supervisor on duty commits suicide by throwing himself under the wheels of a train. More than fifty cars are involved in a crash at Upminster, England, injuring six people.

Friday An airliner carrying forty-four passengers hits a two-storey house while approaching Albany airport, New York. The crash kills seventeen, and injures thirty-three.

Saturday Two earthquakes cause 100,000 people to flee their homes in Tuzla, Yugoslavia. In a nearby coal mine, two workers die after being trapped 450 feet underground. A Turkish liner, Maremara, catches fire and sinks in the Golden Horn. Three men are electrocuted at a coal mine near Wakefield, England, after their crane, carrying a rail in a high wind, touches a 24,000 volt overhead wire. Five people die after a hovercraft overturns in the Solent, England, during rough seas.

Monday Seventy-five Iranians are reported dead after a lorry overturns attempting to cross a river near Bandar Abbas. Nine explosions in a firework factory near Chicago, USA, destroy the building, kill three people and injure seventeen. Two skiers die in an avalanche in the Tyrolean mountains. A ten-storey block of flats in Barcelona, Spain, collapses, killing at least fifteen people.

Tuesday At least 500 people die from poisoning in the Baghdad area after eating grain treated with mercury. Because of a warning of possible pollution, the water board at Rugby, England, stop drawing supplies from the River Avon, which flows near a waste tip where hundreds of drums of cyanide are said to have been buried. A British sailor is drowned after the coaster Katie-H collides with a fishing boat and sinks off the Dutch coast.

Wednesday A doctor warns that a widely-prescribed anti-depressant drug has caused at least three deformed births in Australia and could be responsible for further deformities. In New York, a pedestrian, after being knocked down by a car, whose driver did not stop, is run over by a further fifty cars, whose drivers also do not stop.

Those seven days, with their thousand or so deaths, are in no way unusual. Any other week in the year would yield a similar result.

Patterns do emerge from any study of disasters, although I leave it to others to estimate their significance.

There is an inevitability about some disasters, a seemingly inexorable working out of a sequence of events, a series of coincidences that fall into place to cause an unforeseen and terrible happening. Time and again, people describe misfortunes in terms of Greek tragedy.

Indeed, some people seem almost to create an atmosphere for disaster by a display of *hubris*, that unreasonable, unreasoning pride that was the downfall of many a tragic hero. A classic individual example was the builder of the first Eddystone lighthouse, who longed to be in residence during a great storm. His wish came true, with one of the worst storms that has ever lashed the British coast. When it was over, he and his lighthouse had gone.

On a larger scale, the owners and builders of the Titanic showed a foolish complacency by insisting that their liner was unsinkable. It sank, of course, at the first opportunity. (One of the survivors, Miss Edith Russell, recently told me: 'I took it as a sign that man can never control the elements'.) In much the same manner, the owners of the Morro Castle claimed that their liner was the safest afloat shortly before the ship burst into flame, and the ill-fated Lakonia was advertized as offering a cruise 'with all the risks removed'.

However, the scenarios for most disasters, involving a dark irony that borders on the farcical, seem less like the work of a Sophocles than something written in a collaboration between Joe Orton and Evelyn Waugh. A naval officer opening the door to a torpedo tube and receiving an unexpected gush of water in his face is pure slapstick—except that when it happened to Lieutenant Woods aboard the submarine Thetis, it led to the deaths of ninety-nine men.

The sudden switch from laughter to tears is evident in such an horrific event as happened in Victoria Hall, Sunderland, on 16 July 1883, when a crowd of children rushed down from a gallery to obtain toys being given away by a conjurer. One child tripped in a doorway, and 186 were crushed to death. Fortunately for my peace of mind, that tragedy from the last century falls outside the scope of this book, although I have given details of a similar accident that occurred at Bethnal Green, London, underground station during World War II.

War as such, and the destruction it causes I have excluded as a subject on its own, although I have mentioned some disasters that happened during war, and which even involved soldiers, such as the two terrible train crashes at Quintinshill and at Modane, since they were not due to enemy action. The sinking of the Lusitania was an act of war, but it falls within my definition because but for the carelessness or worse of those who sent her on her last voyage enemy action could have had no effect.

Most of the worst disasters of the twentieth century are covered, but I have made no attempt to be encyclopediac in my coverage, for that would require a book five times as long. Some, indeed, serve merely as a symbol of far greater disaster that threatens this spaceship earth. Thus I have traced something of the effect of DDT on the environment, and of the Torrey Canyon on the pollution of the sea, but I could as easily have chosen other examples of ecological damage, such as the industrial waste that is turning the Mediterranean into a dead sea.

Most people involved in disasters are overcome by a feeling of helplessness that is often illusory. People become so imprisoned in a way of life that they lose the ability to act. The Appalachian miners of Buffalo Creek Valley knew that the dam at Lorado was weak, but they managed to live with that knowledge for eighteen years before they were drowned. If the workers in a Glasgow factory had insisted on a key to unlock the fire escape door, then twenty-two of them would not have died on a November morning in 1968.

For what is extraordinary is the way people become convinced of their own ability to survive. 'Earthquake, earthquake!' W. C. Fields once yelled, shaking the billiard table so that he could win against Humphrey Bogart. It was an amusing ploy, if you forget the fact that Californians continue to live happily in areas that, before very long, are bound to be devastated by a major 'quake.

Disasters will never be prevented, such is human nature. But they can, and must, be lessened. A great deal of improvement is possible, particularly in the establishment of national, and even international, organizations, to provide warning and relief.

Many catastrophes are predictable, but warnings come too late. If a warning had been sent down the coast during the great storm of 1953 that ravaged the entire east coast of Britain, then many lives could have been saved. In 1966, seven hours before much of Florence disappeared under water, it was obvious that a serious flood was on its way, but no warning was given. Workers at Italy's Vaiont dam were alert to the danger of a landslide on the morning of 9 October 1963. But no one passed on the message to the villagers in the valley below, and 2000 drowned.

Disasters repeat themselves, too, with a frightening regularity. The trouble is, memories are short. But, while people forget, an organization could remember. Only the United States has an Office of Emergency Preparedness in Washington, D.C., ready to cope with disaster situations. If other countries set up the same sort of organization, and also developed a reliable warning system, it would be a valuable step in limiting the scope of disasters.

While much effort is expended in alleviating physical suffering, we still ignore the psychological aspects of catastrophes, the rehabilitation of the victims. There is now plenty of evidence of the traumatic effects that can result from involvement in disasters, the fear and hostility that can poison an entire community. That, in part, is one of the grim lessons of the Aberfan disaster (see page 140). But there is still little official recognition of this.

The development of technology has altered the pattern of disasters which have tended to get fewer but bigger, and beyond the control of ordinary people. As the comedian Godfrey Cambridge said, on being confronted by a jumbo jet, 'I never asked for a two-storey plane.' When the first jumbo crashes, the death toll may reach 500.

Also, we are now in the curious position of being better equipped to watch disasters, with the aid of film and television cameras, than to prevent them.

Indeed, there is a point at which people's natural curiosity, and interest, in disasters shades into a strangely passive morbidity. Any disaster will attract hordes of sight-seers, even when there is nothing to see. They prefer to watch rather than to act. When the Taeyonkak Hotel burnt down in Seoul, there were many dramatic photographs taken of the unfortunate victims, although few lives were saved. Hundreds of people gathered, in June 1969, to watch the burning of one of England's most delightful buildings, the Aldeburgh Festival Hall at Snape, Suffolk. But no one thought to call the fire brigade. Spectators were taking photographs of the event twenty minutes before the fire engines arrived.

We remain quick to help those caught in disasters, and equally quick to forget. Public indignation, though fierce, rarely lasts long enough to force changes and improvements.

We are often satisfied by nothing more than fine-sounding, if empty, rhetoric.

In the accounts that follow, the figures given for the numbers of the dead are, at best, an approximation since accurate counts are rarely available and victims sometimes take a long time to die. There is even dispute about the numbers killed in such a well-documented catastrophe as the sinking of the Titanic.

It is easy to overlook, in the immense suffering involved, that it is individuals, like ourselves, who undergo such unnecessary pain and torment. As that admirable organization, the Red Cross, says: 'Disaster happens to people, one at a time.' The disasters that follow should not have happened to anyone.

1 The uneasy balance: man and his environment

The Cliff House Hotel at the south head of
San Francisco harbour. During the earthquake,
it fell into the sea.

A shattered street of San Francisco.

The Dome was all that remained of City Hall, a building which cost £1,200,000 ($2,880,000).

San Francisco and Tokyo: the once and future earthquakes

The first San Francisco earthquake of 1906 was a natural disaster, an act of God. The second, which will come sometime in the next ten years, will be a man-made disaster, an act of folly.

Ever since it happened, Californians have ignored the earthquake which devastated San Francisco and killed 400, preferring instead to remember it, which they do infrequently, as the Great Fire. They acknowledge the means of destruction, the flames that spread rapidly from one end of the city to the other, but forget its cause, the shift in the San Andreas fault that runs across the state.

Neither San Francisco nor Los Angeles is a safe place to live. Yet the inhabitants of both, hypnotized by the many attractions, remain steadfast in the all-too-human belief that a disaster is something that happens to other people, never to oneself.

It was at 5.13 a.m. on Wednesday, 18 April 1906 that the San Andreas fault shifted and the city's streets began to undulate. The whole city rocked and rolled. The tremors toppled buildings and shattered water mains so that firemen could do little to control the flames that immediately engulfed many of the wooden buildings and saloons.

The 'quake lasted for a minute and in that time shook over 50,000 square miles of California. It split the surface of the earth for more than 200 miles. In places, the rupturing ground tore apart fences by as much as twenty feet. San Francisco's morgue overflowed with dead bodies.

In the confusion that followed, the commander of the local army garrison sent in troops to impose order on the stricken city. Soldiers attempted to limit the fires by dynamiting buildings, which, inexpertly done, caused further havoc and started new fires. The troops were ordered to shoot looters and they blazed away with abandon, even killing, in their zeal, some householders trying to rescue their own possessions.

The fires raged for three days, by which time the city had suffered some

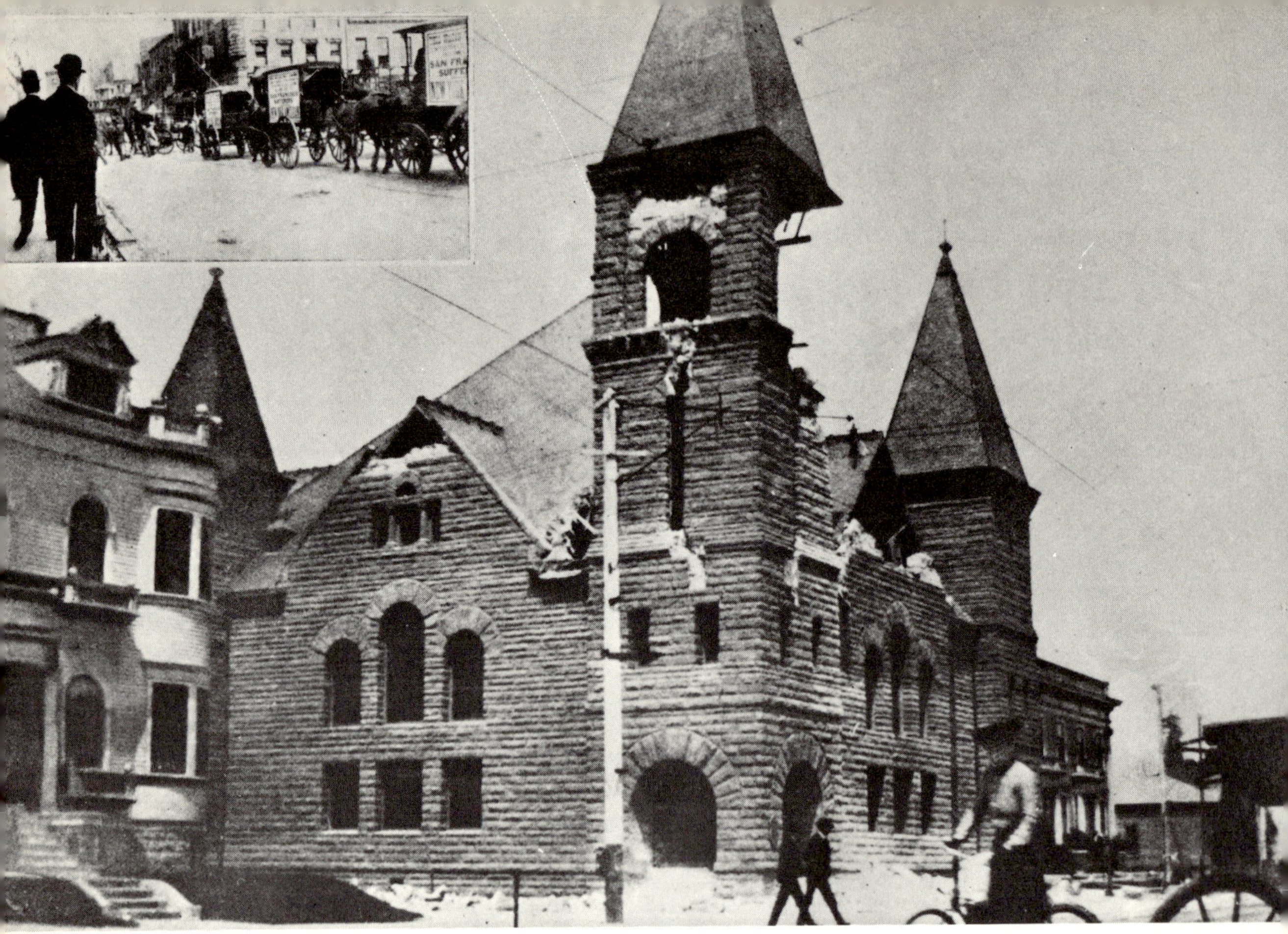

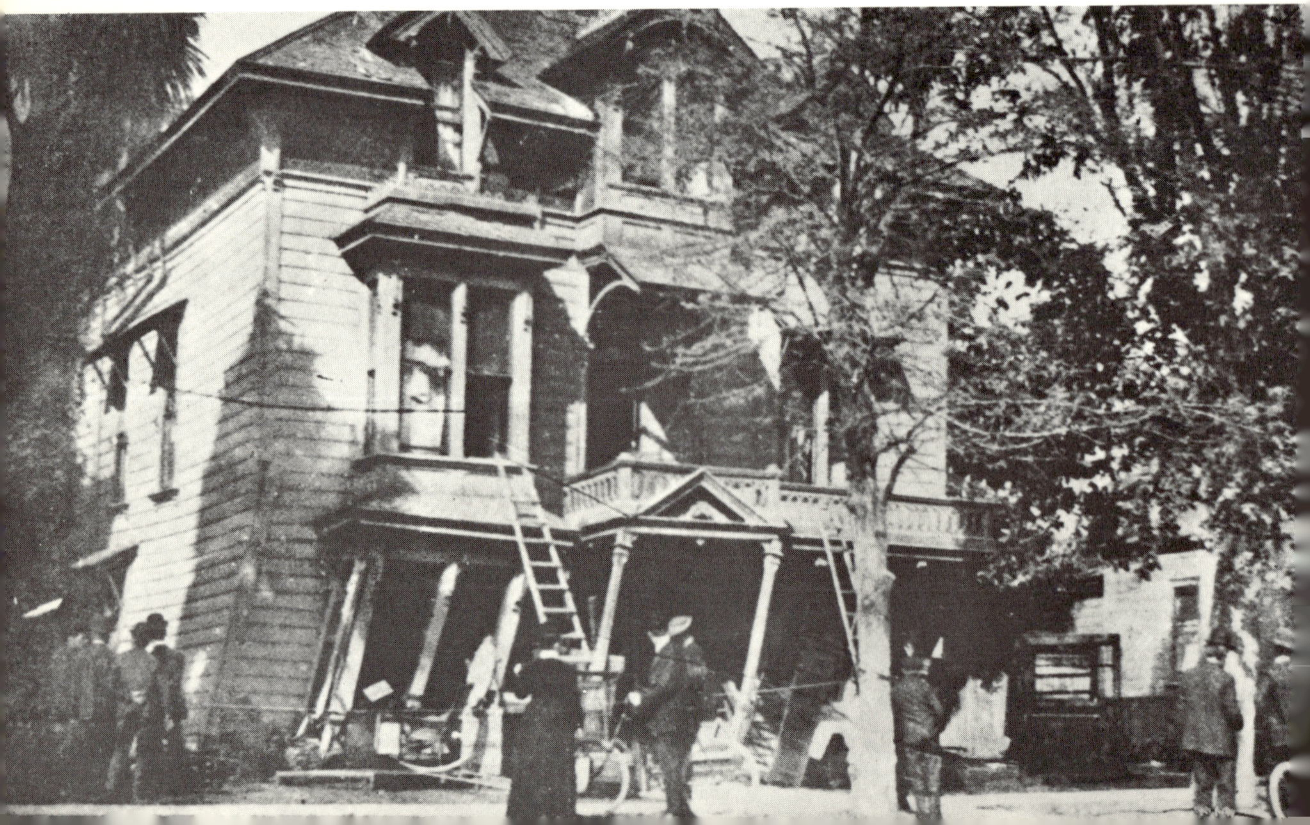

Left the wreckage the earthquake left behind. *Above* the Baptist chapel in ruins (*inset* San Francisco street scene). *Below* a typical wood frame house twisted by the shock wave.

Top the aftermath of the earthquake: San Francisco in flames. *Below* the destruction of the city. The blackened portion of the chart shows the extent of the fire.

$500,000,000 (£192,000,000) worth of damage, and more than 100,000 people were homeless. Since then, San Francisco has grown rapidly, so that estimates of the numbers who will be killed next time range from 100,000 to 750,000, depending on whether the earthquake happens during the rush hours.

Where once low wooden buildings stood, now rear skyscrapers, most of them built with little knowledge of how they will withstand severe tremors. Even more seriously, skyscrapers and public buildings have been erected directly over fault lines. Some of the city's most expensive apartments are in the Bay area which, in a major earthquake, would form a gigantic quicksand.

The Hayward fault runs through such crowded areas of the city as Berkeley and Oakland. There are thirteen schools serving 5000 children built near fault lines, as well as police stations and even a civil defence headquarters. In all, forty hospitals and schools are built on or near a major fault and new building was continuing in such danger areas in the 1960s. There are still no regulations controlling the placement of hospitals, fire stations, and power stations. The city's emergency services are dependent upon the telephone for communication.

East of Oakland, the Briones Dam straddles an earthquake fault and towers over thousands of homes. In Los Angeles in 1971 following an earthquake 120,000 people were evacuated because it was feared that the Van Norman Dam might collapse, loosing three billion gallons of water on a residential area.

Earthquakes are measured on the Richter Scale which progresses logarithmically, so that Magnitude 2 is ten times as great as Magnitude 1. The 1906 earthquake measured 8.3. The Los Angeles earthquake of February 1971 reached 6.5 on the scale.

It is perhaps significant that most of its fifty-six victims died in the rubble of two hospitals, including the US Veterans Hospital at Sylmar, San Fernando, where thirty-eight were killed.

In a sense, California is already a disaster area, for few people are prepared for the future calamity. Nor are earthquakes any novelty. There have been major ones in 1857, in 1933 when 120 died and the seaside resort of Long Beach was devastated, in 1952, and in 1964.

Some scientists have calculated that the two sides of the San Andreas fault slip past each other at the rate of two-and-a-half inches a year. In the San Francisco area, where the fault is locked, the strain built up since 1906 could lead to a sudden slippage of thirteen feet. The San Francisco earthquake may already be overdue.

The activity among the area's seismologists is frantic. They are developing techniques to predict earthquakes and even to prevent them, but it will be a long time before such control is possible.

The present verdict must remain that made by a local newspaper in 1906: 'Present situation: worse. Prospects: gloomy'. The Californians prefer to live in ignorance of their faults.

The Japanese general Araki once told George Bernard Shaw: 'an earthquake for us is both a catastrophe and a form of religious enlightenment for the national spirit.'

If that is so, then the people of Tokyo are due for an excess of religious enlightenment during the next decade, even greater than the blinding revelation of 1923 when Japan was shaken by the most devastating earthquake of this century. It levelled Tokyo and Yokohama and killed probably 150,000 people, although no one had time to count the exact numbers of the dead.

The first shock came ten minutes from noon on 1 September. The Asakusa Tower, 220 feet high, which adjoined the Asakusa Temple dedicated to the Kuannon Goddess of Mercy, collapsed, killing 700 people. Another 600 were buried in the ruins of a three-mile-long railway tunnel. Few died in those early minutes; no more than 2000.

But panic followed, and fire. The flames were fanned by a high wind that carried burning debris across the city to begin new blazes. The small wooden houses burned

The devastation that was Tokyo.

swiftly. The firemen were virtually helpless for the first shocks broke the water mains and also fractured gas mains. In the city's Imperial University Hospital 800 patients burned to death.

The poor, fleeing from the slum areas, took shelter in a military camp. More than 8000 died as it, too, caught fire. Many who had sought refuge in the Ueno Railway station were killed as it burned. Troops only added to the confusion as they blew up houses to contain the fire. A local radio station compressed the horror into a few words: 'It is like hell! Buildings are falling. Fires are blazing everywhere. Streets are strewn with the dead and dying.'

Under the weight of fleeing crowds, bridges collapsed into the river, and others were drowned in canals as they attempted to escape the flames. Tokyo, as well as Yokohama, where 400,000 lived, and some smaller towns were nothing but ashes.

Modern Tokyo is the world's largest city with a population that has increased in fifty years from 1,500,000 to 11,000,000. Like San Francisco, the city is ill-prepared for the next disaster, which cannot be far in the future. The Southern Kanto area, which includes Tokyo, has never gone more than sixty-nine years without a massive earthquake.

Whenever it comes, it will kill around a

million people and again destroy the city, which is not built on the surest foundations. Tokyo sinks between one and eight inches a year and parts of the city are six feet below the level they were in 1945. Some bridges are now too low to allow boats to pass and more than eighty of the city's 810 square miles are below sea level at high tide.

Tidal waves following an earthquake would swamp Tokyo Bay. The city not only has skyscrapers but three levels of subways and underground shopping arcades. No one knows the effect of a severe shock on the elevated expressways, roads, and bridges.

Tokyo does have a Disaster Prevention Centre, which estimates that a 'quake of the 7.9 magnitude of 1923 would destroy fifty square kilometres of the city within ten hours, rather more than in 1923. At least 1200 fires would break out immediately in a city that still contains many wooden buildings and narrow streets. Tokyo has only 1000 fire engines and the first shock waves would inevitably rupture water mains and cause leaks of inflammable gas and oil.

The Japanese have another saying of which they are fond: 'Disasters only take place when you have forgotten about them.' Who remembers 1923?

Britain and Holland, 1953: the tide that waited for no man

It was a stormy January in 1953. In the Irish Sea, the British Rail ferry ship Princess Victoria foundered after waves had battered open the cargo doors at the ship's stern, drowning 128 of the 172 people aboard. On the last night of the month, the worst gale for nearly twenty years raged in the North Sea.

The wind reached speeds of 100 m.p.h., whipping the sea into huge waves that crashed on the coastal areas of Britain, from the Orkney Islands to the Thames Estuary, and also of Holland and Belgium. Rarely has so much devastation been done in a single night.

Even the Dutch, ceaselessly engaged in a battle against an ever-encroaching sea, were unprepared for the height of the tides. They did anticipate flooding, and the country's four radio networks began broadcasting warnings early on 1 February. Even so, the sea won its greatest victory against Holland since the fifteenth century. Some experts claimed that it was unavoidable, the latest in a 500-year cycle of great inundations, although others regarded it as a punishment from God.

At 4 a.m., church bells were rung and ships and factories sounded sirens as the dykes broke and the sea swept as much as forty miles inland. The tide was two feet higher than any ever recorded in Holland and within minutes had breached the dykes in more than sixty-five places.

The island of St Philipsland, where 400 people lived, was totally submerged. On another island, Goeree-Overflakkee in South Holland, 433 were drowned, and rescuers found the bodies of 180 huddled in a barn where they had taken shelter. In places the water was forty feet deep.

Within a day, 605 were reported dead. By

Rowing down the main road. A rescue operation in the flooded streets of Jaywick.

the time the floods subsided, nearly 1800 died and another 300,000 suffered in one way or another, many being marooned for three or four days without drinking water. In Belgium, twenty-two were drowned and the shopping centre of Ostend, which had been newly rebuilt after World War II, was destroyed.

The Dutch used 5000 craft of every kind for rescue work. By the end of February they had closed half of the sixty-eight tidal gaps in the dykes with the aid of 15,000,000 sandbags. On 6 November, as Queen Juliana watched, workers closed the last breach through which water still flowed. The sea defences were as strong as ever, although no stronger.

Winston Churchill spoke about 'the

Canvey Island the day after the floods. With houses still half-submerged, troops work at repairing the shattered sea wall.

unprecedented violence of the sea' that day. Britain was taken completely by surprise, her coastal defences exposed as inadequate, and her communication and warning system as non-existent.

In the howling gale, the sea began to devastate the Wash at 6 p.m. But no one passed on this information. As the jury remarked at an inquest in Rochford, Essex, on sixty-eight people who drowned: 'We feel strongly that the worst consequences of this disaster might have been avoided if warning had been sent down the coast.'

At Southend pier, for example, a tide of seventeen feet four inches was expected. At 11.38 p.m. an alarm sounded as the water reached the danger level of twenty-one feet. Two hours later the tide reached its high point of twenty-four feet seven inches.

At Canvey Island, the sea walls gave way at 1.10 a.m., six hours after the Wash had suffered damage. A tidal wave eight feet high rushed inland, trapping many in their homes. Others who ventured out were swept away in the rapidly rising waters. Rescuers later found bodies wedged in trees. The sea swept away all but three of the bungalows that stretched for one and a half miles along the front at Hunstanton. At Margate, the harbour's stone lighthouse, sixty feet high, was smashed.

Along the Thames embankment the

A macabre reminder. Some of the 2000 sheep killed at Sittingbourne, Kent, impaled on barbed wire after the flood waters receded.

riverside streets of London were flooded to a depth of four feet. In Barnes, a seventy-year-old man, who slept in an air-raid shelter in his garden because he liked peace and quiet, was drowned as it was submerged.

There were miraculous escapes. In Canvey Island, a baby floated safely in a pram for twelve hours. Many won awards for their bravery, including nineteen-year-old Peter Beckerton, who was awarded his posthumously. He waded through waist-deep water to warn a neighbour. He was last seen near the front door, just before the house was swept away.

Britain's sea walls were breached in more than 1000 places. Some 25,000 homes were flooded, and 307 people died. Since that time, little has been done to improve the country's defences. The likelihood of flooding has been increasing for a century in south-eastern England, which is sinking at the rate of a foot a hundred years.

London remains particularly vulnerable. There are plans to build a flood barrier across the Thames at Woolwich, at a cost of £75,000,000 ($200,000,000). But this safeguard, which was first suggested in 1954, is unlikely to be operating before 1978.

Before then, central London could easily flood, disrupting the underground railways system, as well as power supplies and the telephone system. One official estimate is that a serious flood would cause £1,000,000,000 ($2,600,000,000) damage.

Those areas of London which are in danger have made emergency plans, including the use of sirens to warn people living in basements and ground floors to leave their homes. But the chances of a serious flood before the barrier is built are around five to one. The only possible comment was made by a parrot, rescued by firemen in Harwich during the floods of 1953. As they rowed it down the street, the bird jumped up and down in its cage, shrieking: 'Oh my God! Oh my God!'

Florence and Venice, 1966: art in flood

It was a squally, wet November in Italy. Over the Tyrrhenian Sea, a cyclone brought worsening weather. On Thursday morning, 3 November 1966 it began to rain, a steady, hard downpour. In the Dolomites, more rain fell that day than usually falls in six months. It turned the snow to slush, swelling the mountain streams and rivers.

At 10 p.m. that Thursday night, at Levane, thirty-five miles above Florence, the gates of a hydro-electric plant were opened as flood waters threatened to burst the dam. At that moment, it was certain that the River Arno would flood its banks. But no one warned the Florentines as they prepared for bed. Such action, it was felt, might cause a

St Mark's Square, Venice, under water.

A wrecked car swept by the flood into Florence's Piazza Mentena.

general panic, with people attempting to flee from the city in their cars.

Early on Friday, at 5 a.m., the Arno burst its banks and the waters surged into the city, flooding houses up to the level of the first floors and turning two-thirds of Florence into a lake up to six feet deep. The electricity supply failed, telephones stopped working, and drinking water was quickly polluted. In the streets, 20,000 cars disappeared under the water.

Not since 1270 had Florence been so devastated by floods. When the water went down, it left behind over everything a coating of evil-smelling mud mixed with naphtha, the thick oil that had gushed from central heating plants. A few people were happy: the seventy-three prisoners who escaped from the city's main jail through a flood-damaged wall on the first day.

The floods affected a third of Italy, causing 173 deaths and damaging 800 villages. Outside Italy, people's concern was over the grave damage, estimated at a cost of £57,000,000, to Florence's many superb works of art, reminders of the time when the

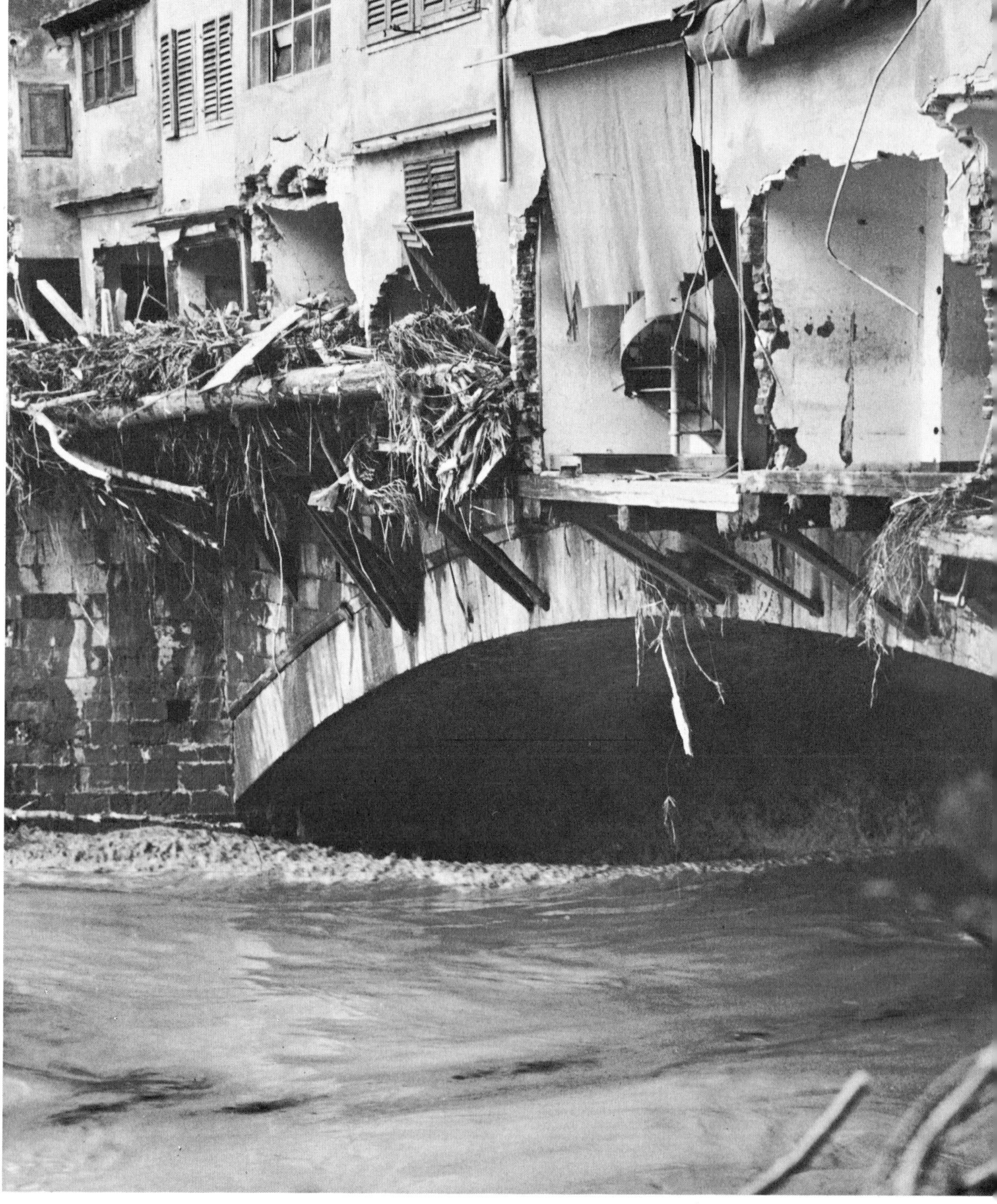

city was the most magnificent and civilized state in the world.

Few great works were lost, but more than 600 paintings were totally destroyed and several thousand damaged. Among those ruined was a crucifixion scene by Cimabue, the great 13th century artist. The force of the flood water tore out of their frame five panels of Ghiberti's celebrated Gate of Paradise in the Baptistry.

In the Biblioteca Nazionale, many thousands of books, magazines, and newspapers were spoiled or destroyed. In the Archaeological Museum, 9000 Greek and Etruscan vases were shattered and other treasures were lost beneath thick mud and slime.

Reaction to the tragedy was mixed. Many countries of the world sent money to pay for the work of restoration. The Archbishop of Florence, who regarded the disaster as of biblical dimensions, thought it was a divine punishment for man's wickedness. The Italian government imposed heavy taxes to raise money and politicians squabbled over who was to blame.

Florence was not the only one of Italy's beautiful and fragile cities, blossoming in stone, to suffer indescribable damage. The dykes that protected Venice from the Adriatic burst and the waters rushed into the city, wrecking 100 gondolas and bringing the worst floods for 966 years. St Mark's Square became an extension of the lagoon and was under five feet of water for twenty-four hours.

Venice's marriage to the sea is no longer a happy one. Its buildings crumble into the lagoon. Its paintings and frescoes decay from damp. Stone and marble disintegrate in an atmosphere polluted by the growing industrial areas of Mestre and Marghera. Sewage pollutes the canals. The city sinks a

Shops damaged by the swirling waters along the Ponte Vecchio, Florence.

centimetre a year as the factories pump out water from an underground lake beneath the Po valley.

The 1966 floods led to the setting up of a centralized organization to deal with national calamities. The government plans to build sluice gates in the Venetian lagoon which would prevent future flooding and also control the high tides that now lap St Mark's Square at least fifteen times a year. Whether either move will be effective will be discovered with the next deluge.

The Ikuta landslide: a slip by experts

There are some disasters that teeter on the edge of farce; events which, in other circumstances, would seem amusing but, because they involve death, acquire a terrible irony.

So it was in Ikuta, Japan, on 11 November 1971, when a team of government scientists from the Agency of Science and Technology set about their investigations into the cause of landslides, which lead to many deaths in the country each year. Their eventual aim was to prevent such catastrophes.

As an experiment, they decided to water a steep loam hillside to simulate heavy rain and so cause a small slide. They invited journalists and television cameramen to watch. Firemen sprayed water from a nearby reservoir on the hill, which was twenty metres high.

Suddenly and without warning, an overhanging cliff crumbled, sending a mass of mud and boulders, three metres deep and fifty metres long, crashing down on the scientists and journalists. The slide was so swift that no one had time to run.

A television cameraman staggered out of the mud still holding his camera containing film of the sudden tragedy, which was shown to Japanese viewers the same day. He was among the lucky ones, for ten people were injured in the landslide and fifteen died, although they had been standing well back from what had been designated the area of danger. The experts admitted that their slide exceeded their expectations.

Rescue workers dig frantically in the thick mud, searching for survivors of the man-made landslide at Ikuta.

Bengal, 1943: 'They that die by famine die by inches'

Bengal is disaster-prone. The people suffer unavoidably, due to such natural and recurring calamities as cyclones. Most of the worst cyclones in history have begun in the Bay of Bengal. In 1970, in one of the most devastating natural disasters of the century, a cyclone smashed across East Bengal, killing 50,000 people. In 1971, another

Starvation is a slow and painful death. A Calcutta street scene.

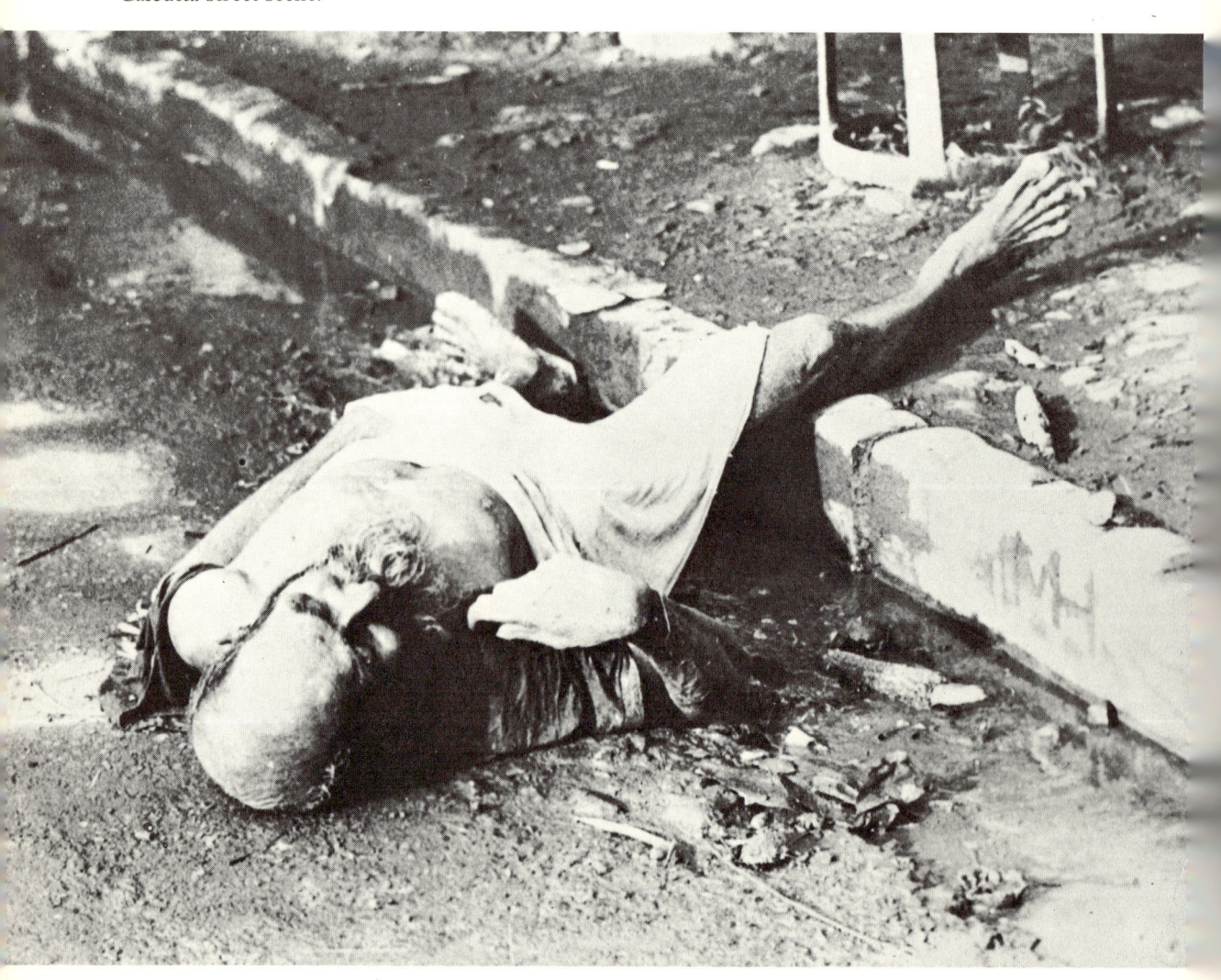

monstrous storm hit India's Orissa State, leaving some 20,000 dead.

But these are nothing to what happens when man aids nature. In 1971, during the war in East Pakistan, more than twenty million people faced starvation, a familiar situation for many. Among the dead were those who had survived one of the worst famines of this century.

It happened in 1943 and was largely ignored by a world busy with war. More than 1,500,000 died. By local standards it was small scale: more than 10,000,000 are estimated to have died from hunger in 1769.

The harshness of the hunger in 1943 caused a total breakdown of normal life. Many killed themselves before they died of starvation and others fell victim to the epidemics—cholera, malaria, dysentery, and smallpox—that followed. Desperate men turned to crime, or sold their wives and children for rice.

A few black marketeers grew rich as they hoarded and then sold food at inflated prices. A hurricane destroyed 1,500,000 tons of rice and aided profiteering. In 1938 Bengal's 53,000,000 people ate an average of 344 lb. of rice a head at a cost of 0.4p (1.04c) lb. In 1943 the population, risen to 60,000,000, ate an average of 290 lb. of rice a head at a cost of 1.8p (4.68c) lb.

The British administration did little to help. They continued to allow the export of food from Bengal although, because of the war, the usual import of rice from Burma was cut off. They took little notice of warnings of a likely food shortage and relief supplies, when they came, were not distributed properly.

The war took priority. Their policies were dominated by the fear of a Japanese invasion. This led them to take over the country's boats—more than 20,000 were impounded—so that the people could neither fish nor carry supplies of food along the rivers.

In Calcutta and other cities, the starving and the dying who had made the journey from the barren countryside in search of food littered the streets. Along the approach roads, too, the dead lay in countless numbers.

The Torrey Canyon: oil on troubled waters

When the explorer Thor Heyerdahl sailed across the Atlantic on his papyrus raft Ra II, he found that the ocean was polluted by oil for forty-three out of the fifty-seven days of the journey. The moral is clear: we can no longer think of the sea as some vast and bottomless deep, able endlessly to absorb human waste. It is vulnerable and already dangerously contaminated.

The British scientists who studied the disaster when the giant oil tanker the SS Torrey Canyon went aground concluded that not only were we lucky to get off so lightly, but that similar, even more menacing accidents were highly likely.

They estimated that Britain would face another incident involving a giant tanker within ten years, and that the coastline would be seriously polluted three or four times a year. Other areas of the world are in as great danger, for oil tankers are involved, on average, in two potentially serious accidents a week.

In 1965 the Liberian tanker Otto N.

The broken remains of the Torrey Canyon, held fast on Seven Stones reef.

Miller collided with the Norwegian ship Nora ten miles off Britain's Beachy Head and 2600 tons of oil escaped into the sea. Every year, some 500,000 tons of oil ends up in the oceans, much of it from the cleaning of the tankers' cargo compartments. As the scientists reported, after studying the effects of the Torrey Canyon: 'It is a sobering thought that each thousand tons of crude oil washed on to a beach thirty feet wide could form a layer half an inch thick for twenty miles.'

It was at 8.50 a.m. on Saturday, 18 March 1967 that the Torrey Canyon, carrying 119,000 tons of crude oil from the Persian Gulf to Milford Haven, smashed on to Pollard Rock, part of the Seven Stones reef in the English Channel, sixteen miles west of Land's End, the extreme south-west tip of England.

The tanker hit the sharp-edged rocks at a speed of sixteen knots and was ripped open for more than half of its length, in some places by fifteen feet of jagged rock. Of the ship's sixteen tanks, only two were undamaged. Within a few hours, the sea was contaminated by 30,000 tons of oil. For twelve hours, until the pumps failed with the flooding of the ship's boilers, the captain ordered that more oil should be pumped out in a vain attempt to refloat the tanker.

The pollution was on a scale that has never been equalled, although it cannot be long before it will be. By Thursday, when there was a fleet of twenty-four ships continually spraying detergent on the troubled waters, another 20,000 gallons of oil had escaped. Eight days after the disaster, a gale put an end to salvage attempts which had resulted in the death of a Dutch seaman.

After the bombing, the tanker burns with black, oily smoke.

In the storm, the tanker's back broke, spewing a further 50,000 gallons of oil into the sea. That spring, there were the highest tides for more than fifty years along the Cornish coast. The surging waters carried 20,000 tons of oil high on to beaches from the Lizard to the north of Newquay. Some 1400 men worked to clear the mess, using detergent lavishly and removing, in places, a top layer of sand a foot deep.

Meanwhile, the British Prime Minister, Harold Wilson, overreacted causing much cynical amusement. He ordered that the Torrey Canyon should be bombed to burn the oil that remained in her tanks. In one raid, ten days after the ship had gone aground, Royal Naval Buccaneer strike aircraft dropped forty 1000 lb. high explosive bombs. RAF Hunter fighters jettisoned 5400 gallons of fuel from their under-wing tanks to help along the fire and also used rockets and napalm bombs on the wreck.

In the cleaning-up operations, 2,500,000 gallons of detergent were used, most of it at sea. The detergents which were most efficient in dispersing the oil were also the most poisonous to marine life, and killed many crabs, lobsters, and plant life.

The French, faced with the same problem, used sawdust to sink oil slicks and removed the contaminated sand from the beaches.

North-westerly winds drove the oil first to Guernsey and then to Brittany, where it began coming ashore on 9 April and continued for the rest of the month until there was a continuous deposit, up to a foot deep, for sixty miles from the Baie de Lannion in the west to the Pointe de L'Arcouest in the east.

They also tried to use polythene foam to absorb the oil on the sea, but were unable to recover the floating particles which ended up on the beaches. The oil underwent an unpleasant sea-change, coming ashore with the appearance and consistency of chocolate mousse. The French used mobile steam cleaners to remove it from rocky areas. The last of the slicks reached the Bay of Biscay by early June, where the French navy sank it with powdered chalk.

In all, the disaster was less than had been feared, and localized enough to encourage complacency about the future dangers of oil pollution.

Some Breton oyster beds were polluted and the breeding caves of seals contaminated. There was widespread damage to marine flora and fauna, caused as much by the detergent as the oil. It was the sea birds that suffered most. Of the 7849 birds that were rescued and cleaned of oil, only 450 were still alive by mid-April. Altogether, more than 20,000 guillemots and 5000 razorbills died.

DDT: From miracle to menace

DDT, Dichlorodiphenyltrichloroethane, that remarkably effective insecticide developed in 1939 by the Swiss chemist Paul Muller, who won a Nobel Prize for his work, is first among the ecocatastrophes of our time.

In the last twenty-five years, some thousand million people have been freed from the risk of malaria due to its deadly effectiveness in killing mosquitoes. Yet its side-effects are even more spectacular and their disastrous consequences were ignored or suppressed for a long time. When, in 1962, Rachel Carson pointed out the dangers in her now-classic book *Silent Spring*, she came under bitter attack, her integrity was questioned, and pressure was put on her publishers to withdraw the book.

DDT persists in the body. This dangerous quality causes a chain effect, a poisonous escalation of the sort that killed bird life at the Californian resort of Lake Clear, where a closely-related insecticide, DDD, was sprayed to kill mosquitoes. In the water, the concentration of DDD was a minute .015 parts per million. In the microscopic life, the diatoms, in the water, the amount increased to five parts a million. In the fish, it reached ten parts and over. In the lake's Western Grebes, the birds that fed on the fish, there was a concentration of 1500 parts a million, and they died.

The effect of DDT on wild life is varied but inevitably disastrous. Birds of prey, including the bald eagle, the national emblem of the United States, have been made sterile throughout Europe and North America. The brown pelican virtually disappeared from California after the female birds laid eggs with shells so thin that they broke them as they tried to hatch them. Fish in many game lakes have ceased to breed, and the level of DDT in the Pacific and Atlantic Oceans is now nearly enough to upset the reproduction of fish there, too.

There is scarcely a creature in the world without a concentration of DDT in its body tissues. It can be found in the fat of polar bears in the Canadian Arctic, and in penguins far from civilization in the Antarctic. It can be found in sea birds that feed on fish in the open sea and only visit land to breed, evidence that the oceanic food chain is contaminated. Most dangerous of all, very small traces of DDT—as low as one part per billion—can prevent photosynthesis, the oxygen-producing process, in planktonic algae, those microscopic plants vital to life in the sea.

In America, researchers have found the insecticide in the foetus and other tissues associated with birth. The average American has twelve parts a million in his body, nearly twice the level at which meat is judged unfit to eat, and he can take in twice the safe level of DDT with his mother's milk. Smokers can even inhale it from tobacco.

The long-term effects of this are both difficult to estimate and terrible to contemplate. At the worst, DDT could poison the oceans, destroying all marine plant life, turning the waters into dead seas and upsetting the balance of oxygen and carbon dioxide in the atmosphere. Certainly, even if it were never used again, the level of DDT in the world's oceans would continue to rise for many years.

To insects and animals, fishes and bats, DDT brings death. In experiments, it has caused stunted growth in rats and deformed births in mice. It is a direct nerve poison, may cause cancer, and could cause behavioural disturbances to humans as it has to animals. Indeed, DDT has been held responsible for liver damage and degeneration of the nervous system, a trend which, in two or three generations, could result in the birth of imbecile children with damaged brains.

Despite the irreversible ecological damage that DDT has caused, its many powerful supporters believe that it is essential for the control of malaria. Most governments have found it impossible to ban its use.

But its effectiveness, according to the latest evidence, is diminishing as more and more insects—at least 200 species at the last count—become immune to it. In 1971, two DDT sprayers went through the small Brazilian farming town of Altinho during a plague of crickets. The only effect was to make people vomit. A long-scale study of a malaria eradication programme in Central America was launched in the mid-1950s. By 1971, the incidence of malaria, after an initial decline, had risen to figures as high as before due to the mosquitoes' resistance to DDT, while the residues of the insecticide in food were more than ten times higher than the average in North America.

2 Appointments in Samarra: travelling to death

Rail

Carriages blaze fiercely after the triple train crash at Quintinshill.

The Quintinshill crash: a forgotten train

James Tinsley, a slightly built, fair-haired man, was late for work on Saturday, 22 May 1915. He did not mind. He was often late, although he should have been taking over the signal box at Quintinshill, just outside Gretna Green, Scotland, at 6 a.m.

He had an arrangement with his mate, George Meakin, who was then working the night shift at the signal box, to come on duty half an hour late so that he could enjoy a little while longer in bed.

Tinsley, who had been a signalman for eight years, since he was twenty-four, hitched a ride on a local train at 6.10 a.m. It reached Quintinshill at 6.33, and he took over at the box five minutes later. It was a busy time, but his mind seems to have been on other matters. For, although he had ridden on the local, he then forgot all about it, until it was too late.

There was an up and a down line at Quintinshill, and two loop lines. On the down loop that morning, there was a goods train. On the up loop, there was a train of empty coal waggons. The train on which Tinsley had come to work was switched from the down to the up line to allow through an express train to London.

Instead of going home after finishing work, George Meakin settled down to read

After the crash at Quintinshill.

the morning paper. He did not hear the call that came through at 6.43 a.m., when Tinsley was asked if he could accept a troop train further down the line. Tinsley, forgetting all his lines were occupied, accepted the train.

Meakin was just going home when he saw the troop train steam by at forty m.p.h. 'What have you done?' he shouted. What Tinsley had done was send the troop train along the same line as the waiting passenger train. 'I forgot about the local train', he said later.

The troop train had 500 men aboard, soldiers of the Royal Scots Regiment. The head-on crash sent both engines and their carriages toppling over. Hardly more than a minute later, as dazed survivors wandered along the tracks, the express train thundered down, hit the wreckage strewn across the tracks and overturned.

The fire from the engines set the carriages ablaze and, aided by the slight breeze, the flames engulfed all the trains. The fire around the three engines, which lay close together, was so fierce that firemen later were unable to extinguish it.

First to reach the accident were the caretakers of the famous blacksmith's shop at Gretna Green, where so many eloping couples had married. The devastation was so immense that they thought it was an act of war and that the Germans had invaded Scotland. Many passengers were burned alive and two men had their legs amputated to save them from the flames.

The dead numbered 227, with 246 injured, far surpassing the previous worst rail accident of the century when twenty-eight died at Elliot Junction in December 1906 and, indeed, the worst to that date, when seventy-three drowned during the Tay Bridge disaster of 1879.

Most of the dead were soldiers, although it was impossible to tell how many since identification was difficult and the regimental roll call had been burned. Some of those listed as missing turned up later during the fighting at the Dardanelles.

As for Tinsley and Meakin, they were arrested and put on trial, after an enquiry had established that their clandestine arrangement for a late start to the day shift was responsible for the accident. Meakin was sentenced to eighteen months in prison, and Tinsley to three years. Both men gave way under mental strain during their jail terms, suffering nervous breakdowns, and they were released after serving a year.

Modane, 1917: the runaway train

Two of the most serious-ever railway accidents have involved troop trains. The crash at Quintinshill, Scotland, was the worst in Britain. That at Modane, France, on 12 December 1917 was the worst in the world.

The French soldiers, 1025 of them, were returning home for a few days leave after fighting in Italy. Two trains had been coupled together to form one, nineteen carriages long. The troops were crammed in, as many as fifteen to a compartment.

From Modane, a small town in the mountains of Savoy, by the border with Italy, the railway track goes downhill. Soon after steaming out of the station, the train began to run away along rails made slippery by frost. Its brakes would not hold against the huge weight, some 520 tons, of coaches behind. Slowly at first, and then quicker and quicker, the train picked up speed until it was completely out of control.

At first, its weight kept it on the rails. But, as it sped along, another hazard threatened. The brake blocks began to grow ever hotter with the friction until they set alight the wooden floors of the carriages. The flames were fanned by the rush of air as the train clattered ever faster down the track.

It became only a matter of time before the wheels jumped the rails. First, the engine broke away from the rest of the train, a circumstance that saved the life of the driver. Then, past the Pont des Saussaz, which spans the River Arc, where the line curved somewhat sharply, the leading carriage left the track to smash into a high wall, with the rest of the train crashing behind it at a speed of more than ninety m.p.h.

The fire swiftly spread throughout the wrecked carriages, aided by innumerable small explosions from the grenades and shells that the French soldiers were bringing back as souvenirs of the war. There have been varying estimates of the number of dead. Only 425 bodies were identified. The lowest figure for those killed is 543, although some claim that the correct figure is 560, and others put it at more than 800. Whatever the right number, the crash remains the most devastating of all rail accidents, and is still commemorated in an annual service at the village of Saint-Michel-de-Maurienne, where the bodies of the dead were taken.

Immediately after the crash, the engine driver was arrested, although he had done everything to prevent a disaster which he had foreseen. Before the train left Modane, he complained about the brakes. Only the first three carriages were fitted with air brakes. The rest relied on ineffective hand-brakes. He had demanded air brakes on all the coaches, realizing that the size and weight of the train would make it impossible to control on the steep downward slopes ahead.

But there were no other coaches available. As the second troop train had not arrived on time, the train was already two hours late in leaving Modane. He was ordered to take out the train. With no alternative but to attempt the journey, the driver had set off at a snail's pace. His caution was not enough to prevent the brakes from failing. The driver was, however, the obvious scapegoat and had to face a court martial, where he was acquitted. His superiors, who had insisted that the train should leave at once, overriding his objections, do not appear even to have been reprimanded. The dead were casualties of a wartime impatience and the attitude of *laissez-faire* that so often afflicts men in positions of power when faced with a potentially disastrous situation. More than most they seem inclined to ignore the odds and to believe in a continuing good fortune.

The Lagny crash: when everything fails

It was two days before Christmas, 1933, and the express from Paris to Strasbourg was packed with travellers making their way home for the celebrations. The train was so crowded that many had to stand in the corridors with their suitcases bulging with presents.

There were Christmas crowds, too, laden down with luggage on the train from Paris to Nancy. The day, Saturday 23 December,

38

was a chill one and also foggy. For this reason, the Nancy train had left Paris two hours later than scheduled. The Strasbourg express, a later train, was also delayed an hour at Paris.

About fifteen miles from the capital, the Nancy train came to a halt in the dense fog just outside the small town of Lagny, almost a suburb of Paris. The signal was at danger. The crew, playing safe because of the thick fog, ensured that there were detonators along the track behind them to warn any other train approaching them down the same track.

The Nancy train then began to move cautiously forward. Despite their precautions, the Strasbourg express thundered down the line to smash into them at a speed of more than sixty m.p.h. The express was hauled by a massive locomotive, weighing some 150 tons, and made up of heavy steel coaches, so that its total weight neared 600 tons.

The Nancy train was of older, flimsier stock. The carriages were made of wood. In the moment of tremendous impact, the express totally demolished the other train's guard's van and continued on to plough through four carriages, reducing them to splinters. The passengers, packed tight in the fragile compartments, had little chance to escape.

There were 230 killed and another 500 injured. In the dark and the thick, chill fog, the rescue work went on slowly. Bonfires were lit from the shattered fragments of the carriages. When a breakdown train arrived from Paris, it lacked both spotlights and tackle for lifting clear the heavier pieces of wreckage.

The driver of the Strasbourg express had missed somehow the signal that had checked the Nancy train. Apart from the visual signals there was also an aural one, a buzzer that sounded in the driver's cabin, operated by a device set between the rails at the signal point. On this occasion, the electrical contact had failed, put out of action by the freezing fog.

The detonators, too, had failed to go off on time. Passengers in the last coach of the express heard them explode, by which time the driver was out of earshot.

Other disturbing factors were revealed. Not the least was that the express driver received a bonus for punctuality, a system that led inevitably to risks being taken. Both he and his firemen claimed that the signals on the line were often incorrect, and that they had made official complaints about this in the past. The day before the accident, the automatic signalling system in the express had gone wrong. Although it was repaired, it does not seem to have been functioning properly.

As worrying as the fact that every aspect of the signalling system seems to have failed at the same moment, was a statement made by M. Dautrey, director of France's State Railway. He pointed out that they still had 1000 of the old wooden carriages in regular use, and that only seventy-five miles of the State Railway's total of 5700 miles was equipped with automatic signalling. It was, he said, a habit for the French to put off spending money for as long as possible.

The crush at Bethnal Green: a short trip

The underground railway station at Bethnal Green, in London's crowded East End, made an ideal air raid shelter. And so it became during World War II, providing a refuge for more than 5000 people at a time.

On Wednesday, 3 March 1943 a warning siren sounded as German bombers began to fly across England for a bombing raid on the capital. Immediately, people in the area left their homes and made their way through the blacked-out streets to the shelter.

The approach to the shelter was also badly lit, with just a dim light burning halfway down a flight of nineteen steps that led from the street to a landing. As they neared the station, some people wondered whether the doors had been opened for there had been an occasion in the past when they had been forced to wait on the stairs for the doors to be unlocked.

About 2000 people were in the shelter, with a steady stream moving down the steps when a woman, middle-aged and carrying a baby and a heavy bundle, tripped on the seventeenth step. Burdened as she was, she could not stop herself sprawling on the dark landing. Walking just behind her was an elderly, balding man. He tripped over her and fell, too.

After that, it was like a chain reaction. The man behind him tripped and fell and those behind him did the same, and the ones behind them. As the crowd continued to move down the steps, more and more fell over each other. It was too dark to see properly, and the shouting and scuffling sounded to those higher up the steps as if the doors had not been opened yet. Indeed, some people were heard to shout that the doors were locked.

In a few minutes, the entire staircase was blocked by fallen, struggling bodies, with more and more people, walking down in an inexorable tide, adding to the scrimmage. The steps, unlike those at some other stations, lacked a central handrail which might have saved some from falling.

There were 300 people lying packed in that dark space at the bottom of the stairs before anyone realized what had happened. Of them 173 died from asphyxia, including sixty children. Said an eyewitness at the inquest: 'In a moment or two there were dozens of people falling.'

No one seems to have panicked before the woman fell. (She, incidentally, lived although her baby died.) There had been at least one complaint, from a doctor, that the stairs were dangerous. But the official inquiry into the accident was held in private and the government decided that, as it was wartime, it was not in the national interest to publish the findings.

Many fantastic rumours sprang up to explain the accident. They led the Home Secretary to tell Parliament that the report 'dismisses as without foundation the rumours that the accident was caused by a Jewish panic or induced by Fascists or criminals for nefarious purposes.'

But, if there was no stampede, no panic, was one woman falling enough to cause the deaths of so many? All that the Home Secretary would say was that the accident was due to 'a fortuitous combination of circumstances'.

Certainly, there was no reason for any panic at the shelter that night. Although other parts of London suffered some heavy damage during the raid, the nearest bomb fell two miles away from Bethnal Green.

The Balvano tragedy: choked to death

It is no coincidence that many of the worst railway accidents have happened during wartime, for it is at such periods that standards are inevitably lowered and risks taken, since people live with the knowledge that they may die at any moment, and that tends to liberate their actions.

So it was at 5 a.m. on 2 March 1944 as a long goods train of forty-seven wagons snaked slowly out of the small halt of Balvano, high in the mountains of the Lucania district of Italy. The wagons were mainly loaded with illegal passengers, hitching a ride. They had swarmed aboard as the train chugged slowly away from the station, up a steep incline.

They were a motley collection, a few peasants and local farmers, but mainly the jetsam that a war throws up: deserters, petty criminals, and black marketeers, all anxious for an easy ride over the mountains.

There were two engines pulling the long train of wagons. In them, the firemen grumbled about the quality of the coal, another result of the war. It was poor grade stuff that burned badly, giving off little heat and a great deal of thick, black smoke.

The train chuffed slowly up the steep track, on occasion almost coming to a halt.

It may have been due to the unexpected weight of the passengers, but the train did finally shudder to a stop soon after entering the long uphill tunnel that burrows through Mount Armi.

It was at this moment that a misunderstanding seems to have arisen between the drivers of the two locomotives. One thought it best to get up as much steam as possible and continue through the tunnel. The other wanted to roll the train backwards, out of the tunnel. Between them, they ensured that the train remained stuck where it was.

It was all over in a few seconds. Both the drivers and their firemen were quickly dead, poisoned by the high carbon monoxide content in the black smoke still pouring from their funnels. The deadly cloud rolled back through the tunnel, choking the passengers who were trapped like cattle in the wagons.

Only those at the rear of the train, which was still in the sweet, mountain air survived. The news of the tragedy reached Balvano from a brakeman who ran back down the line as soon as he realized what was happening. But the rescuers were too late. In the Armi tunnel, 509 people had choked to death.

The Harrow crash: an inexplicable error

Train driver Robert Jones spent his day decorating his house and then went to bed early, at 7.45 p.m. Because the regular driver was on holiday, he was scheduled to take over the Perth-London express at Crewe on the morning of 8 October 1952. It was foggy, and the train was thirty-two minutes late in arriving.

At 4.37 a.m. he left Crewe and drove carefully towards London through the thick fog. Later, it lifted although there were still a few misty patches. Driver Jones had been cautious, and his train was running more than eighty minutes late by the time he reached the outskirts of London.

He was approaching Harrow and Wealdstone Station when something inexplicable happened: he took his express through a signal at caution. He should have cut his speed. The signal was a bright one and ought to have been visible for at least four seconds.

But, somehow, he missed it. Judging by a post-mortem, he was not taken ill. Nor was there anything wrong with the engine to distract his attention. A passing freight train may have blinded his view, but it seems unlikely.

He also managed to miss two semaphore signals set at danger, but these were harder to spot. It is likely that he was unsure of his exact position, although he had been over the route thirty-eight times before, that he was looking out for the signal he had missed when he saw ahead of him Harrow station, and realized his error.

Driver Jones died with his hand on his emergency footplate brake. But nothing could stop the express, roaring into the station at sixty m.p.h., smashing into the rear of a commuter train, which was beginning to move away. It mounted the other's carriages, travelling on for many yards before it overturned, stopping the station clock at 8.19 a.m.

At that moment, an express, bound from London to Liverpool and Manchester, came through the station at sixty m.p.h., ploughing straight into the wrecked carriages of the other trains that lay across the rails. A fourth train was stopped 300 yards from the station.

The triple crash killed 112 and injured 349 people.

The tangled wreckage of the three trains that crashed at Harrow. In the background can be seen the station clock which stopped to give the time of the disaster: 8.19 a.m.

43

Sea

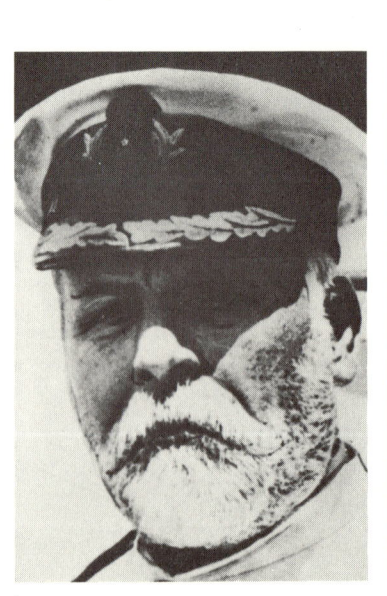

Above the Titanic in all her glory. *Below* three of the men who died aboard her: Isadore Strauss, Captain E. J. Smith, the liner's commander, and millionaire John Jacob Astor.

The Titanic: an unthinkable calamity

The Greeks had a word for it. They called it *hubris*, which they defined as an overweening pride, a fatal flaw in a tragic hero. The English talk of pride going before a fall. Certainly, the maiden voyage of the Titanic provided a classic example of hubris, of the truth of the maxim.

As much as World War 1, the Titanic disaster marked the end of the Edwardian era, the golden age for those rich enough to enjoy it. The casualty list told a privileged story. Of the 322 first class passengers, 130 died.

Of the 276 in the second class, 161 died. Of the 708 in the third class, 532 died. There were twenty-nine children travelling first or second class. One died. In the third class, fifty-three children were drowned, and twenty-three saved.

As it was put at the inquiry, sixty-three per cent of the first class passengers were saved, forty-two per cent of the second class, and only twenty-five per cent of the third class. In later disasters, death became far more democratic.

The Titanic was more than the biggest liner in the world: 104 feet high, 852 feet long, and weighing 46,328 tons, a vast floating luxury hotel. To her owners and builders, she was a symbol of man's final superiority over the elements. This complacency was shared by nearly everyone. The first newspaper report after the disaster carried the headline: 'All Saved From Titanic After Collision'. And, at the moment when more than a thousand people were drowning in the Atlantic, the vice-president of the White Star Line was still telling reporters: 'We place absolute confidence in the Titanic. We believe that the boat is unsinkable.'

A few people lacked such absolute faith. One passenger, Miss Edith Russell, who still survived in 1972 at the age of ninety-two, had a premonition that the liner would sink and, just before sailing, wrote a letter full of her fears to her secretary. There were other, stranger premonitions too. In 1898, Morgan Robertson had written a novel in which a liner, filled with rich and complacent passengers, hits an iceberg and sinks. The liner was named the Titan. Six years earlier, W. T. Stead had written a story, 'From the Old World to the New', about a perilous transatlantic voyage through icebergs. He wrote: 'The ocean bed beneath the run of the liners is strewn with the whitening bones of thousands who have taken their passages as we have done, but who never saw their destinations.' Stead, then the most famous British journalist, went down with the Titanic.

There were many other distinguished passengers who paid £870 ($2250) to travel on the maiden voyage. Among the millionaires aboard, whose combined bank balances were said to total more than £120,000,000 ($310,000,000), was Colonel John Jacob Astor, returning to America from his honeymoon, Bernard Guggenheim, who had made a fortune in mining and smelting, and Isadore Strauss, noted for his philanthropy, who was alone worth £10,000,000 ($26,000,000).

Such was everyone's confidence that the liner carried only the regulation sixteen lifeboats, capable of holding only 1178 of the ship's 2207 passengers and crew. The captain, sixty-two-year-old Edward J. Smith, who traditionally took the White Star liners on their maiden voyages, believed that modern shipbuilding had reached the stage where disasters could no longer happen. His actions bore out his dangerous confidence.

For the Titanic was steaming at full speed towards an ice-field which had drifted a long way south from the Arctic across the route to America. Captain Smith received his first warning of the dangers ahead on 12 April from a French liner, the Touraine. By the morning of Sunday, 14 April, three other liners had sent warnings to the Titanic.

The last came that evening from another White Star liner, the Californian, whose captain, Stanley Lord, had decided to shut down his engines and drift because of the number of ice-floes. But when the Californian's wireless operator got through to the Titanic, he was told to get off the air. The Titanic's operator was busy sending out messages for the passengers.

The temperature had dropped sharply on Sunday, as the great liner, still steaming forward at twenty-two knots, neared the ice-field. Captain Smith posted some lookouts in the crow's nest. It was, as the survivors later described it, 'a cold, star-lit night'. Visibility was excellent and the sea was calm and as flat as a billiard table.

At 11.40 p.m. there was a signal from the crow's nest to the bridge that something was directly ahead. It was followed by a telephone call to say that it was an iceberg. There should have been just enough time for the liner to steer clear of the iceberg. But somewhere, between the crow's nest warning the bridge and the bridge giving instructions to the engine room, there was a delayed reaction, a few seconds were lost—enough to ensure, at the speed with which the liner was moving, that the Titanic was ripped open under water for some 300 feet by the razor-sharp ice.

The iceberg was enormous. 'It was so big it seemed to fill the sky', remembered one of the crew. Later, some of the passengers claimed that they had noticed it twenty minutes earlier. It seems odd that the lookout saw it only seconds before the crash, on such a clear night. An explanation for this has been put forward recently by a German doctor, Heinrich Wietfedt. His theory is that the look-out was suffering from night-blindness due to a diet deficiency common in a time of hardship and deprivation for the working classes.

Although the liner was doomed from the moment of collision, the passengers took little notice of the fact. Miss Russell remembers making snowballs from the ice that scattered the deck on her way to bed. 'We thought it was a great joke,' she remembers. The shock seemed a small one. To the second officer, then in his cabin, it felt no more than 'a slight grinding'. Even when lifeboats were being lowered, some passengers showed a marked reluctance to leave the sinking ship. The first lifeboat, which held forty, went away with only twelve on board.

The end of the Titanic, depending on one's viewpoint, was either sublime or ridiculous. Bernard Guggenheim and his valet changed into their evening clothes so that they could die like gentlemen. Some of the crew spent their last hours trying to save the mail, for there were more than 3000 mailbags aboard.

Captain Smith attempted to keep up morale by telling everyone: 'Be British'. One of the British officers, giving evidence at the inquiry in America, explained how he had fired his revolver to prevent some of the steerage passengers from jumping into his lifeboat as it passed them. 'I saw the Italians and the Latin people on the lower decks as we came down, all glaring and ready to spring,' he said. Indeed, almost until the end, the crew tried to prevent third-class passengers from entering the first-class boat deck.

The ship's band gallantly played on, with renditions of hymns, such as *Nearer, My God To Thee* and, finally, the recessional hymn *Autumn*. Mrs Strauss refused to leave in a lifeboat, insisting that she be allowed to stay with her husband, Isadore, to whom she had been married for forty years. The devoted couple died together. Even after the captain gave his last order—'every man for himself'—releasing the crew, the wireless

The Titanic's lifeboats being lowered seventy-five feet from the liner's deck to the water. An artist's impression.

↓ 75 FEET FROM BOAT DECK TO WATER.

operator remained at his post.

At 2.20 a.m. on 15 April 1912 the Titanic slid beneath the waves, taking with her 1503 people. Those in lifeboats nearby feared that they would be swamped by the suction as the liner disappeared, but a series of three underwater explosions pushed their boats out of danger. Among those who escaped on the last boat was Bruce Ismay, chairman of the White Star Line, who never recovered from the effects of the disaster. He retired to Ireland, where he lived as a recluse until his death in 1937.

According to the survivors, there were many examples of selfless behaviour. Captain Smith rescued a small child and handed her into a lifeboat before disappearing to his death. Swimming figures would approach an upturned boat or some wreckage and, learning that there was no room for them, would bless the survivors, wishing them luck before throwing up their arms and drowning. But most of the lifeboats took care to steer clear of the struggling mass of people in the water.

There seem to have been two ships in the area that could have saved most of the Titanic's passengers. One has never been satisfactorily identified, although it has been suggested that it was a Norwegian seal-catcher which steamed away because the captain thought he was under observation for fishing illegally. And there was the Californian, which made a belated arrival after another liner, the Carpathia, had picked up all the survivors.

The official inquiry, by the Board of Trade, censured the Californian's captain, Stanley Lord, for ignoring the Titanic's distress rockets when lying no more than ten miles away. To the end of his life, in 1962, Captain Lord claimed that he was made a scapegoat and that his liner was much further away. In recent years, two attempts have been made to persuade the Board of Trade to re-open the inquiry in order to clear Captain Lord's name, but without success.

But, even giving Captain Lord the benefit of the the doubt, his behaviour was far less admirable than that of Captain Arthur Rostron, of the Carpathia, who picked up the Titanic's SOS fifty-nine miles away and zig-zagged to the rescue through the icebergs at seventeen knots, the highest speed the liner ever achieved.

A statement formulated by a committee of the survivors spelt out the reasons for the tragedy of the Titanic:

> In addition to the insufficiency of lifeboats, rafts, etc., there was a lack of trained seamen to man the same (stokers, stewards, etc., are not efficient boat handlers). There were not enough officers to carry out the emergency orders on the bridge and to superintend the launching and control of the lifeboats, and there was an absence of searchlights. The Board of Trade rules allow for entirely too many people in each boat to permit the same to be properly handled.
>
> On board the Titanic, the boat deck was about seventy-five feet above water, and consequently the passengers were required to embark before the lowering of the boats, thus endangering the operation and preventing the taking on of the maximum number the boats would hold.
>
> The boats at all times to be properly equipped with provisions, water, lamps, compasses, lights, etc. Life-saving boat-drills should be more frequent and thoroughly carried out, and officers should be armed at boat-drill.
>
> A greater reduction in speed in fog and ice, as the damage if a collision actually occurs is liable to be less.

In May, 1912 passengers on another White Star liner came across a macabre reminder of the tragedy. On the spot where the Titanic sank, they saw an open lifeboat containing the bodies of two sailors and a man in evening dress. In the boat were relics—rings, watches, children's shoes—of companions who had died and been cast overboard.

Despite the fact that explosions as she sank may have torn the Titanic apart, in 1966 the Titanic Salvage Company was formed in

Britain with plans to refloat the liner once its resting place has been located, two miles beneath the Atlantic. The company is headed by Douglas Woolley, who hopes to prove such theories as that a torpedo, fired from a German submarine, put the Titanic's rudder out of operation, and that many steerage passengers were locked behind iron gates to prevent them crowding into the lifeboats.

The sinking of the Lusitania: forewarned is not forearmed

Few of the passengers aboard the Lusitania as she lay in New York harbour on Saturday, 1 May 1915 took much notice of an advertisement in the newspapers, placed by the Imperial German Embassy. It began: 'Travellers intending to embark on the Atlantic voyage are reminded that a state of war exists between Germany and her allies and Great Britain and her allies.'

The message was clear, for three months before the Germans had begun their submarine blockade of Great Britain.

There were other disquieting signs. Some passengers claimed to have received warnings by telegram. And, on the quayside, postcard sellers offered pictures captioned 'The Last Voyage of the Lusitania'.

The liner must have seemed safe. It was the fastest in the Cunard fleet, 762 feet long, and carrying 1257 passengers and 702 crew. The captain appeared confident. He ignored the Admiralty's instructions to steer clear of trouble by keeping to a zigzag course and avoiding headlands, the elementary procedure for evading submarines.

Because of fog and reduced speed—as an economy measure only eighteen of the ship's twenty-four boilers were in operation—on 7 May at a little after noon the Lusitania steamed through the smooth sea off the Irish headland, the Old Head of Kinsale.

At that moment, there arrived in the area the German submarine U-20, returning home after operating off the west coast of Ireland. For an hour it followed the liner until the captain changed course and began a procedure to establish his exact position which required him to keep to the same course for half an hour. The change brought the Lusitania sailing directly towards the U-20.

When the gap between them had narrowed to 400 yards, the submarine commander ordered a torpedo to be fired. At that range, it was impossible to miss. The Lusitania sank swiftly, within twenty minutes. There were 900 people still inside her as she slipped beneath the waves, with the sound of a single, mournful, drawn-out cry.

Many of the passengers were at lunch when the torpedo hit. None of them had been given any instruction in the use of life-belts and some died because they put them on incorrectly. The number of dead was 1198, including 124 Americans, which had a good deal to do with United States' decision to enter the war. Winston Churchill thought that the sinking of the Lusitania and the invasion of Belgium were the two events that ensured the defeat of Germany.

The Germans justified their action by claiming that the Lusitania carried a cargo of arms, which the British denied. Probably the Germans were right, for some survivors reported an explosion on the side of the liner away from that which was torpedoed. It

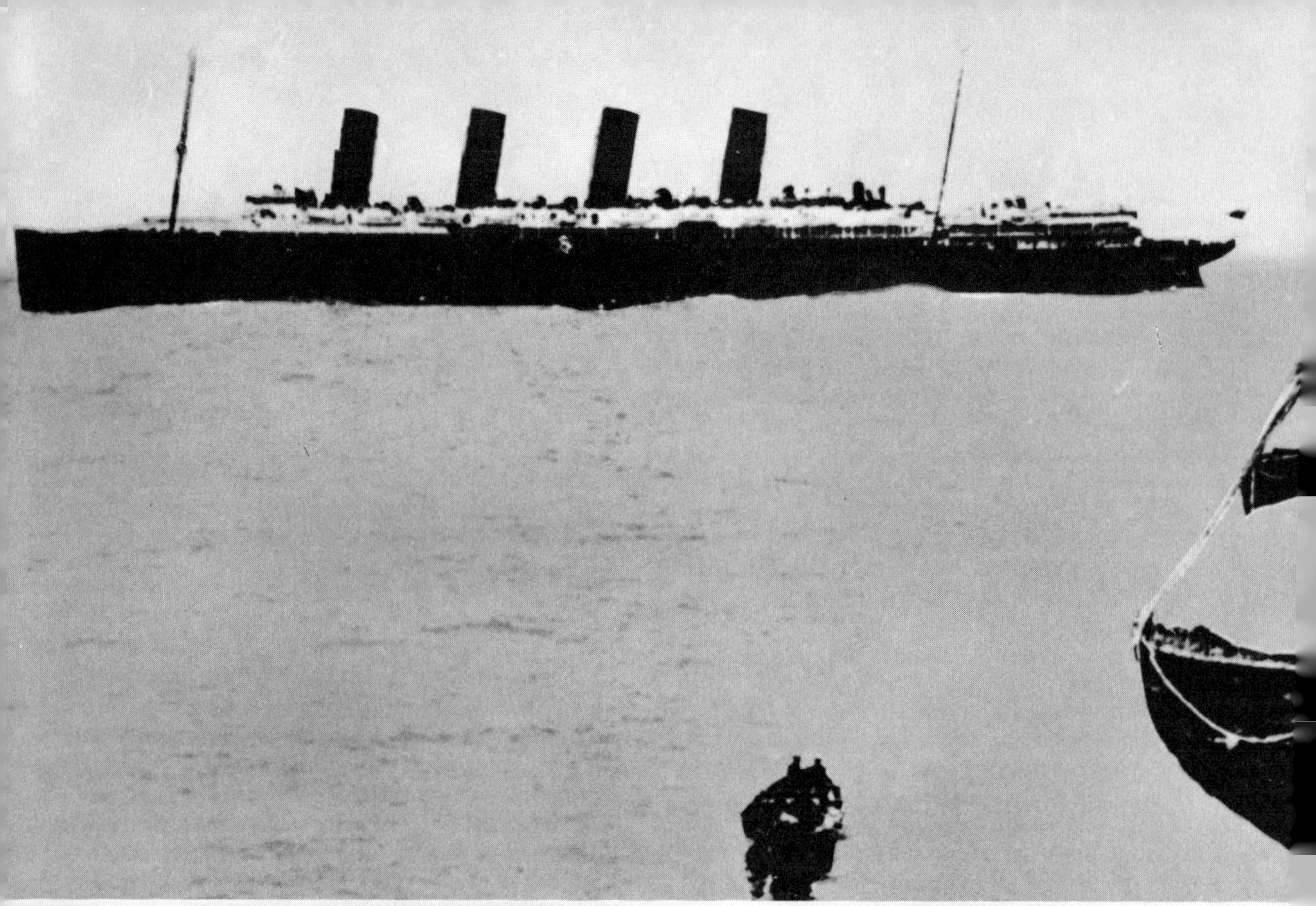
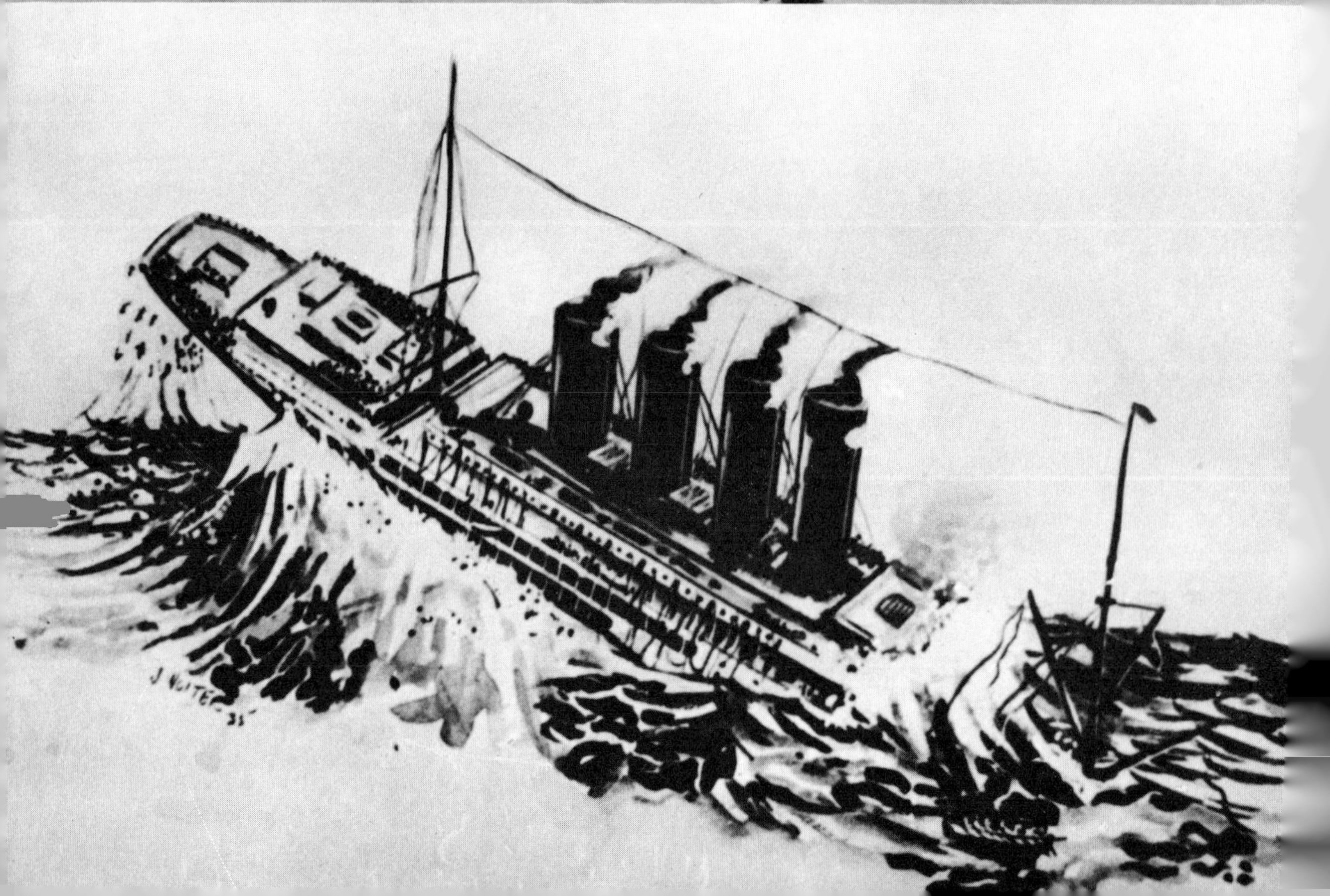

Above the Lusitania. *Below* an artist's impression of the liner sinking.

The German Lusitania medal. *Left* above the representation of the sinking appear the words 'No contraband' and below 'the great steamer Lusitania sunk by a German submarine, 8 May 1917'. *Right* the reverse of the medal shows Death selling tickets in the Cunard Shipping Office and the motto 'Business before everything'.

The final moments of the Lusitania. An artist's impression.

would help explain why she sank so quickly.

Less likely is the accusation that the Lusitania was deliberately sent on a suicide course in order to force the United States into the war, even if this theory would provide an explanation of the captain's reluctance to carry out submarine avoidance in an area where three ships had been torpedoed in the preceding forty-eight hours.

Both sides took advantage of the tragedy for propaganda purposes. The Germans struck medals to commemorate a victory, the British to blacken an enemy. In cinemas in Britain and the United States a virulently anti-German cartoon film was shown. In the Irish village of Cobh, County Cork, where a memorial to those that died on the Lusitania took forty years to complete, the locals' immediate reaction was to smash the shop windows and burn the belongings of a pork butcher who happened to be of German birth.

At the inquest in Kinsale, the coroner brought in a verdict of 'wilful and wholesale murder before the tribunal of the civilized world' against the submarine officers, Kaiser Wilhelm II and the German government.

The Lusitania still lies in 315 feet of water twelve miles off the Old Head of Kinsale, resting in the sand on her starboard side, defying attempts in recent years to salvage her.

The Empress of Ireland waiting at the dockside.

The Empress of Ireland: foggy, foggy death

A terse telegram sent by the ship's captain summed up the tragic end of the steamer the Empress of Ireland, at 1.30 a.m. on 30 July 1906, in the St Lawrence River: 'Stopped dense fog struck amidships vital spot by collier Storstad.'

The Storstad, a Norwegian collier, indeed struck a vital spot. She ripped open a hole of 350 square feet below the Empress of Ireland's water-line. The river poured in swiftly, at a rate of 263 tons of water a minute, so that she listed before the crew could launch more than a couple of lifeboats. Following the Titanic disaster, the ship's owners had ensured that there were enough lifeboats to take every passenger.

Although rescue boats left Rimouski, ten miles away, immediately after the accident happened, when they reached the spot they found nothing remained of the Empress of Ireland but a little wreckage floating on the water. She had sunk within fifteen minutes.

Of the 1367 aboard, 1023 died, twenty-two of them in hospital. The survivors were lucky to escape further injury when the train taking them to safety was derailed shortly after leaving Rimouski.

The accident, decided a royal commission, was the fault of the Storstad which changed course—ported her helm, to use the naval expression—during the fog, carrying her directly across the path of the Empress of Ireland, whose captain had decided to stop the ship until visibility improved. Had the Storstad kept to her original course before the fog fell, there would have been no disaster.

Strangely, there had been a similar accident at the same spot two years before, between a sister ship of the Empress of Ireland and a collier. On that occasion, the roles were reversed: the Empress of Britain had rammed the collier Helvetia, which rapidly sank.

The Morro Castle fire: a villainous hero

Thousands of Americans made their way to the seaside resort of Asbury Park, New Jersey, during the evening of Saturday, 8 September 1934. Once there, they found that the beach and the Convention Hall, with its pier, were fenced off. Gladly they paid an entry fee to stand and stare.

The attraction was the still-burning hulk of the liner the Morro Castle, aground on a sand bank near the pier. They watched the buzz of activity that surrounds any disaster.

They saw dead bodies being washed ashore, for of the 318 passengers and 231 crew aboard, 134—90 passengers and 44 crew—died. Those who arrived early enough, before the dawn, were even able to rob the bodies as they lay stranded on the beaches.

So intense was the interest of the public that it made a national hero of George Rogers, the liner's fat radio officer who had sat, with wet towels wound round his head, sending out SOS messages while equipment in the

THE "MORRO CASTLE" DISASTER:
RESCUE SHIPS STANDING BY THE LINER: PASSENGERS SAVED; THE GUTTED SHIP ASHORE.

THE BURNING "MORRO CASTLE" BETWEEN THE RESCUE SHIPS "MONARCH OF BERMUDA," A BRITISH LINER, WHICH SAVED 71 (LEFT), AND "ANDREA F. LUCKENBACH" (RIGHT): A PHOTOGRAPH TAKEN FROM THE "CHESTER."

A PHOTOGRAPH TAKEN FROM THE "MONARCH OF BERMUDA": THREE LIFEBOATS FROM THAT BRITISH RESCUE SHIP STANDING BY TO SAVE PASSENGERS, SOME OF WHOM ARE SEEN LEAVING THE "MORRO CASTLE'S" STERN BY ROPE LADDERS.

THE "MORRO CASTLE" AFTER SHE HAD BROKEN AWAY FROM TOWING TUGS AND HAD RUN ASHORE AT ASBURY PARK: A PHOTOGRAPH SHOWING THE GUTTED LINER WITH SOME OF HER LIFEBOATS UNLAUNCHED; AND THE CROWD ON THE BEACH.

THE "MORRO CASTLE" WITH THE FLAMES SWEEPING OVER HER AFTER-PART, THE SCENE OF THE GREATEST DESTRUCTION: A PHOTOGRAPH TAKEN FROM THE FORD TANKER "CHESTER," WHICH STOOD BY.

THE BLAZING LINER, AS SEEN FROM THE AIR: A PHOTOGRAPH ILLUSTRATING THE COMPARATIVE SAFETY OF THE BOWS, WHERE THE ACTING-CAPTAIN AND THIRTEEN OF THE CREW, STICKING TO THEIR SHIP, REMAINED UNTIL SHE WENT ASHORE.

The Morro Castle fire. The photographs show different views of the blazing ship, with passengers making their escape by lifeboat and, *centre left*, the liner aground at Asbury Park where it attracted large crowds of sightseers.

radio room exploded from the heat and leaking acid blistered his feet. For a time, he made a living appearing on stage shows and lecture halls re-telling the story of what happened aboard the Morro Castle during the night of Friday, 7 September.

What did happen is still a matter of conjecture. For Rogers proved to be more villain than hero. He was a murderer and may have been something of a pyromaniac. The tragedy of the Morro Castle began with the curious death of the ship's captain, a man who had threatened to sack Rogers, and ended in a fierce and inexplicable blaze.

The ship's owners publicized it as the safest afloat, with an automatic fire detection system and an abundance of fire-fighting equipment. Friday was the last night of the voyage from Havana to New York and included the usual festivities, except that the captain decided to dine alone in his cabin. As he ate a melon, he complained of violent pains in his stomach. An hour later, he was found lying dead and half-undressed in his bath.

At 2.50 a.m., smoke was seen pouring from a ventilator, and a fire was traced to a locker in the ship's writing room, where there was no fire detection system. Within half an hour, the ship was ablaze. The behaviour of most of the crew was marked by cowardice and incompetence. Many had signed on for the pleasure to be had in Havana after the short trip. Some, it was alleged, even paid for their jobs because they could make fast, easy money smuggling drugs into America.

The bo'sun was drunk and unable to organize the fire-fighting team. The first officer, who had taken over command of the liner, for some reason delayed sending an SOS for fifteen minutes, by which time other ships had seen the blaze and sent out calls for help. He kept the Morro Castle sailing at almost full speed, around nineteen knots, into a storm and a high wind which helped fan the flames.

The crew lowered the lifeboats with no regard for passengers' safety. The chief engineer left on the first boat to be lowered, with seven others aboard. The boat would have held seventy. On another boat were sixteen of the crew and no passengers at all.

The first officer and the chief engineer were later sentenced to jail for negligence but, on appeal, they were exonerated.

Rogers' later career was bizarre. He opened a radio repair shop which was not a success. One night, it burned to the ground and he collected the insurance. In 1936, he joined the police force in Bayonne, New Jersey, as assistant to the officer in charge of the radio repair room.

Coveting his superior's job, Rogers tried to murder him with a homemade bomb. He succeeded only in blowing off the fingers of his victim. Rogers was convicted of attempted murder and sent to prison. While in custody, he was asked about the Morro Castle fire and advanced the theory that it was started by an incendiary fountain pen, rigged with a delayed action device, which had been left in the writing room.

In 1942, he was paroled and, eleven years later, murdered an elderly couple to whom he owed money. It turned out that he had a record of petty crime, theft, and assault dating from when he was twelve.

Rogers was capable of poisoning the captain of the Morro Castle and of setting fire to the ship, just as he probably set fire to his own shop. He had the knowledge to make an incendiary fountain pen just as he tried to kill his police chief with an explosive fish tank heater. But did he?

The captain's death, though untimely, may have been from natural causes. An alternative explanation of the fire is that it may have been caused by the overheating of the ship's funnel which passed behind the writing room.

George Rogers was the only one who could clear up the mystery. And in 1958, in New Jersey State Penitentiary, where he was serving a life sentence, he died, refusing to discuss the Morro Castle affair.

The Lakonia fire: removing the risks

The brochure for an eleven-day Christmas cruise from Southampton aboard the Greek liner, the Lakonia, was enticing: 'A holiday with all the risks removed', it promised.

On the third day, towards midnight on 22 December 1963 a fire started in the barber's shop, small enough at first not to trigger the detection system. It may have been caused by a cigarette end, or by a short circuit in one of the many electrical appliances, or by spontaneous combustion among the many cosmetics in the cupboards.

The blaze spread rapidly, so that by the time the alarm did sound the flames were already fierce, burning brightly with the alcohol of the aftershaves and other lotions, and causing poisonous fumes. In an attempt to control the fire, the crew broke open simultaneously doors at opposite ends of the room—one leading to the barber's shop, the other to a hairdressing salon—creating a through draught.

From that moment, there was panic, fear, and incompetence, combining to provide classic conditions for disaster.

Although there had been a demonstration of the safety drill, no officer had ensured that all the passengers turned up, and many had not done so.

No one had explained how to put on a life-jacket. No one had told of the precautions necessary when jumping from a ship into the sea. Several passengers who leapt from higher decks were killed.

No one urged passengers to keep on their clothing before jumping into the Atlantic and then to lie still in order to conserve energy. Even members of the crew stripped off before jumping into the chill waters and swam about frantically in an effort to keep warm. A British doctor estimated that many of the 113 who died of exposure could have been saved if they had known what to do.

None of the officers supervised the lifeboats and, instead, passengers, some of them hysterical and incompetent, took charge. Four lifeboats went up in flames, and, after the last boat had left, there were still 240 people aboard the Lakonia. Some passengers died in their cabins, for no one warned them

Above
Abandoned by passengers and crew, the burning Greek liner Lakonia drifts in the Atlantic.
Below
A close-up of the Lakonia, showing the damage caused by the fire.

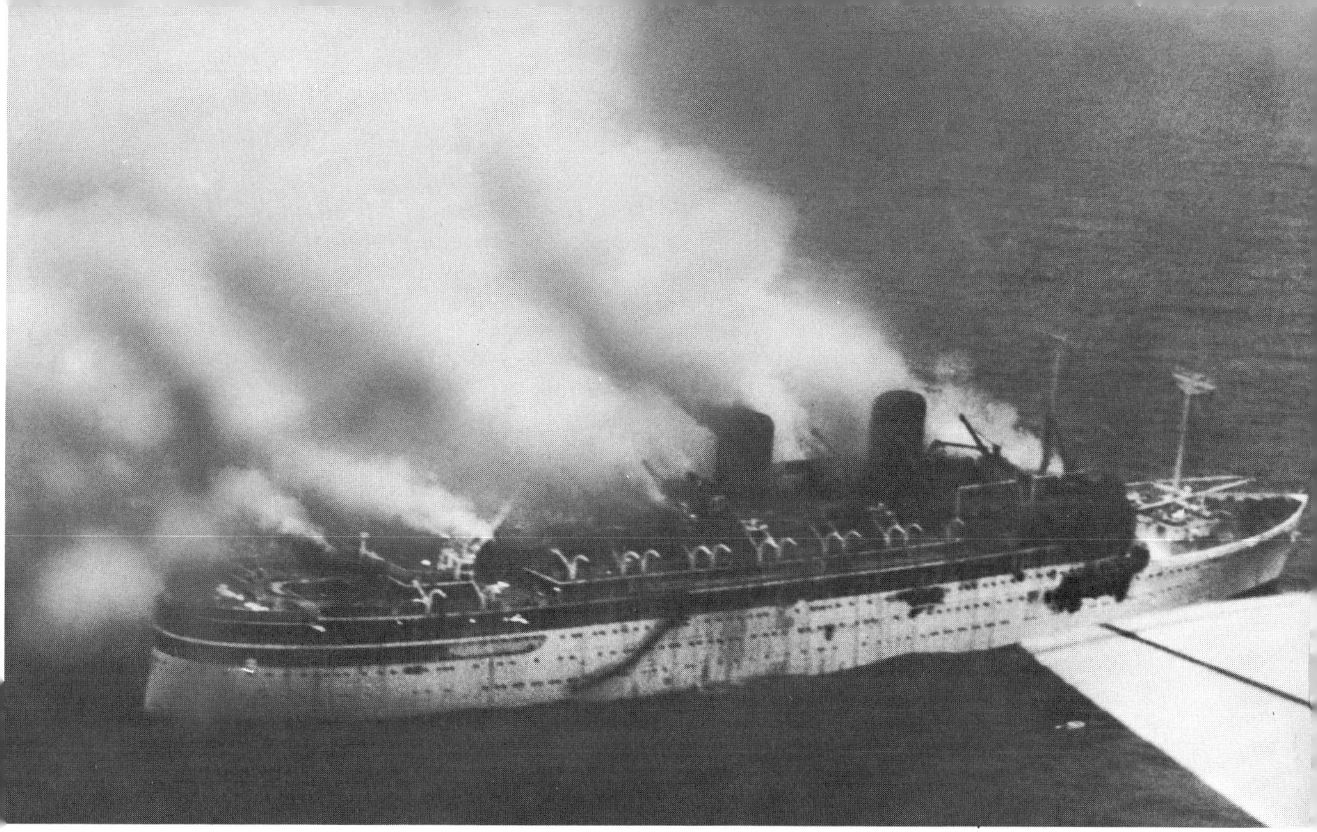

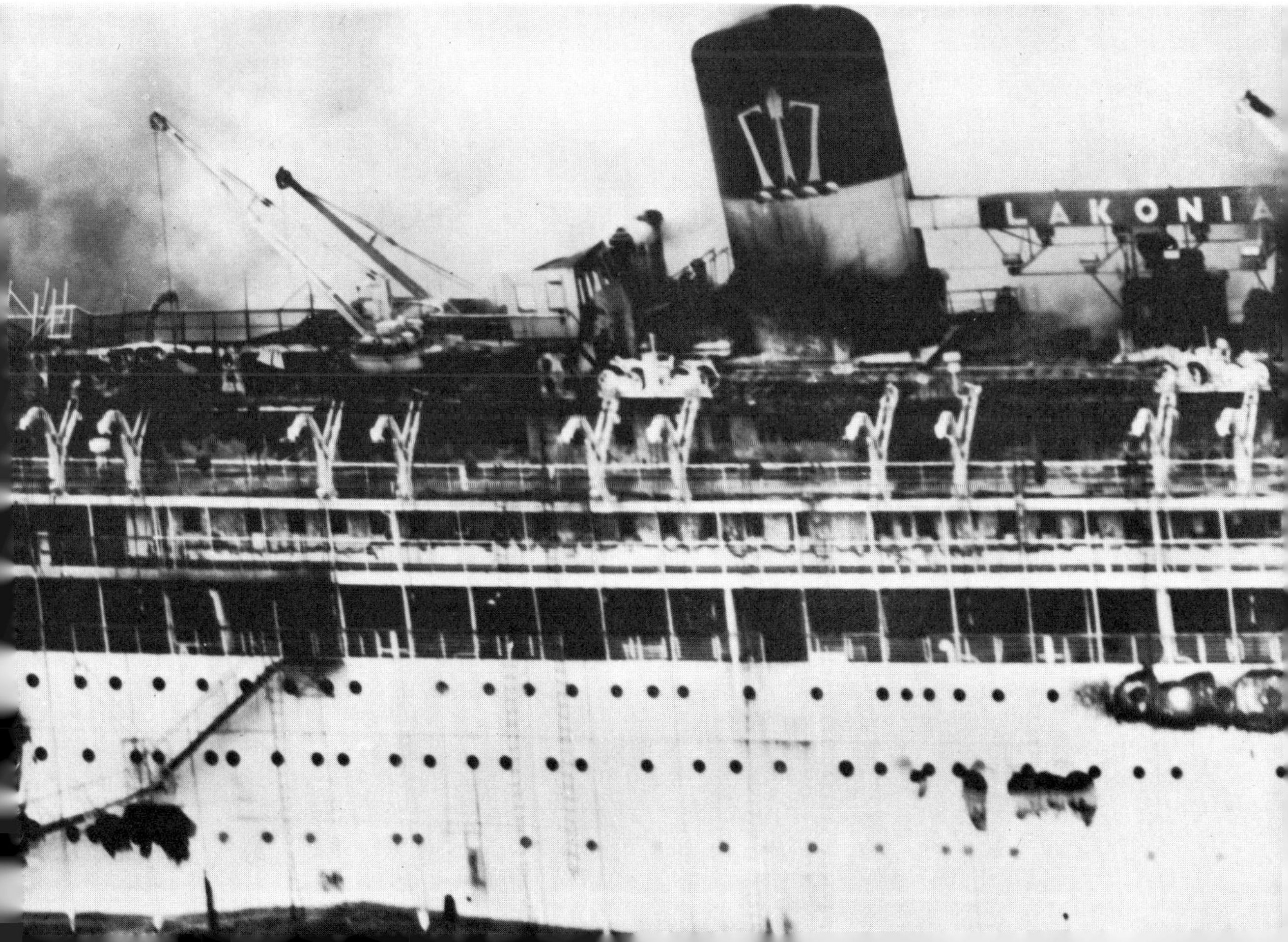
LAKONIA

of the danger and the ship's loudspeaker system failed shortly after the fire started.

The lifeboats that did get clear had no motors and drifted helplessly. There were two motor lifeboats, but neither was in working order so that no one was able to pick up survivors in the sea. In all, 121 died.

The Lakonia's captain and six of his officers were found guilty of gross negligence by a commission set up to investigate the disaster by the Greek government. But, in the ensuing court case, five were acquitted of charges of manslaughter. The captain and his first mate were found guilty.

The Thetis: a tragedy of errors

It was a tragedy of errors, an unfortunate combination of circumstances, that killed ninety-nine men aboard the submarine HMS Thetis in Liverpool Bay, England, on 1 June 1939, a calm and sunny day.

The submarine had forty-one civilians aboard in addition to the usual crew, for she was on her trials. She was behaving oddly. When the captain tried to take her down for the first time, the Thetis merely wallowed ungracefully on the waves.

In the torpedo tube compartment, Lieutenant Frederick Woods checked his buoyancy plan which showed that tubes no. 5 and no. 6, empty of torpedoes, should be filled with water to compensate for the missing weight. He checked the valve of no. 6, and a little water dribbled out. He tried the valve of no. 5. No water at all.

What he could not know was that, during the construction of the Thetis, the hole in the valve had been enamelled over, completely blocking it. He decided to open the rear door of tube no. 5. Through another mischance, an inexplicable one, the tube's bow cap was open to the sea and below the water line. As Woods and the seaman who was helping him tugged open the door, water cascaded through. The Thetis settled in the sea like a steel duck, its head down, its tail eighteen feet above the water at an angle of thirty degrees.

No one—except the unfortunates aboard the Thetis—showed much alarm. The Admiralty announced that there was enough oxygen on the submarine for thirty-six hours, although they should have known that, because of the extra civilians aboard, there was air for eighteen hours only. The first rescue ship did not arrive for several hours.

This was attributable, according to the Tribunal of Inquiry: 'Partly to the absence of any reason to suppose that such a strange accident would happen, partly to a desire not to cause unnecessary alarm, and partly a reluctance to set a number of ships and men in motion as required by the procedure laid down in such a case if it proved to be a false alarm.'

Attempts to secure the tail failed and the Thetis finally settled on the bottom of the sea in less than 150 feet of water. The submarine's captain, together with Lieutenant Woods, was the first to escape, bringing reports of the situation aboard. Two seamen and two civilians followed them into the escape chamber, but they were drowned there. Only two others escaped.

The submarine itself was later refloated, renamed Thunderbolt and played a lively part in the World War II, sinking two U-boats and bombarding enemy positions. On 13 March 1943 she was sunk for a second time,

Sailors try to fix a line to the tail of the Thetis, to prevent the submarine from disappearing beneath the waves.

with the loss of sixty-three officers and men, by an Italian sloop.

But court cases over the Thetis dragged on until 1946. At first, the builders were held responsible for the tragedy. Then the Court of Appeal reversed that decision and blamed Lieutenant Woods. Finally, on 2 March 1946 the House of Lords decided that no one was to blame. On 27 May, ten weeks after clearing his name, Frederick Woods—by then a Lieutenant-Commander and holder of a DSC won at Dunkirk—died in a car crash at Toulon, France.

The lack of sufficient oxygen meant that no one aboard the Thetis was capable of thinking clearly. Had this not been the case the simple solution to their predicament might have occurred to them. An expert submariner, Lieutenant-Commander Alastair Mars, came up with the answer in his novel *Arctic Submarine*, published in 1955.

All that was necessary was the reversal of the pressure in the ship's telemotor system, the hydraulic method, using oil, for remote control of the submarine. The supply and return pipes could have been interchanged at the telemotor panel in the control room.

The reversal would have meant that all machinery with levers at 'open' would have shut and machinery with levers at 'shut' would have opened. This would have closed the bow cap at no. 5 tube and opened the others. As the rear doors of the other tubes were closed, the flooding would have stopped, the water could have been pumped out, and the Thetis would have surfaced normally.

The Affray affair: the case of the broken snort

Someone, deep within the British Admiralty, may know what happened to HMS Affray and her crew of seventy-five immediately after she submerged some thirty miles south of the Isle of Wight on the night of Monday, 17 April 1951. But no credible explanation has ever been made public.

The first realization that something had gone wrong came on Tuesday morning, when the Affray failed to report her position. The code word 'subsmash' set in motion a sea search. A day later, hopes were falsely raised when another submarine, HMS Sea Devil, picked up what sounded like a series of signals, a repetition of the letter 's', near where the Affray had dived.

The search went on for fifty-nine days, with ships covering 23,000 miles of ocean. As it was about to be abandoned, the Affray was found, thirty-seven miles from her diving position, lying on an even keel in 288 feet of water.

The only visible damage was to the snort, the submarine's breathing tube which extended twenty-six feet above the conning tower hatch. Three feet out of the submarine, the snort had been broken off, perhaps by a ship ploughing over it as the Affray was diving.

Or had the snort just cracked open, letting water gush through into the submarine and drowning the crew, most of whom would have been asleep, before they could attempt escape?

The Admiralty favoured another explanation: that a major explosion in the submarine's batteries had caused a shock wave in the hull, cracking the snort which would then have broken off as the ship hit the seabed. But they produced no evidence to back this assertion. The divers who recovered the snort were ordered to abandon further work before they had a chance to discover how the submarine was lost.

The Affray's snort was subjected to metallurgical tests which revealed that it was below standard and that some of the welding was faulty. Defects were also found in the snort tubes of two other Class A submarines and the snorts of all of them were replaced.

MPs raised questions about the disaster in the House of Commons. Among them was Mr J. P. L. Thomas, Conservative MP for Hereford. Ironically, he found himself delivering the final official word on the Affray, as the new First Lord of the Admiralty, following a change in government. Announcing that further inquiries would not be made, he said that tests on the snort showed that it was capable of standing up to all stresses other than those associated with an explosive shock.

It was the Admiralty line, for which the only evidence there is appears to be in the Admiralty's speculation. As another MP, Captain Ryder VC, asked about the snort: 'Should it not be a cardinal feature of this instrument that it should not break off when under stress at some point which could lead to the scuppering of the ship?'

His question has never been satisfactorily answered.

The USS Thresher: high-pressured death

On the morning of Wednesday, 10 April 1963 the nuclear submarine USS Thresher made a routine deep dive beneath the blustery surface of the Atlantic Ocean, some 220 miles off Cape Cod. She was accompanied by the Skylark, a submarine rescue vessel.

After ninety minutes, at 9.12 a.m., the Skylark received a message: 'Experiencing minor problem . . . have positive angle . . . attempting to blow.' The Skylark asked for course and position. There was no reply. The Skylark tried again: 'Are you in control? Are you in control?'

There was two minutes silence, followed by a garbled message from the Thresher, in which the only distinct words were '. . . set depth'. The first word might have been 'exceeding'. It was followed by the muffled sound of the Thresher breaking up. Aboard her was a crew of 129.

At the point where the Thresher dived, the sea is 8400 feet deep. The submarine was designed to cruise at 1000 feet. Below that level, the water would exert enormous pressure on the submarine, reaching eleven millions tons at the sea bottom. Any failure that brought the sea flooding in would have been followed by a loss of power, causing the submarine to sink. She would have exceeded her collapse depth within seconds.

Photographs taken of the wreck of the Thresher showed that as it lay on the sea-bed, which it may have struck at a speed of 150 m.p.h., it was ruptured but largely in one piece. A naval court of inquiry decided that the loss of the ship was probably owing to the failure of a salt water piping system in the engine room.

But scientists studying Scotland's famous Loch Ness monster have put forward another theory. In their investigations they came across a phenomenon by which violent disturbances take place below the surface of the loch, in the thermoclime layer of water, due to stresses set up by the wind.

At one end of the loch this causes an accumulation of warm water which pushes down the thermoclime layer. At the other end of the loch, a shortage of warm water causes the thermoclime layer to rise, thus sending violent surges of water racing from one end of the loch to the other. If this happened in the ocean a submarine caught within the surge might well suffer damage.

The Thresher, built at a cost of $45,000,000 (£17,000,000), seemed fated, for it had spent nearly a third of its three-year existence in dock, being repaired and overhauled. It had undergone an overhaul shortly before the disaster.

Two years later, in 1965, senior naval officers giving testimony to a congressional committee in Washington claimed that several nuclear submarines had almost been lost as a result of defects in design and workmanship.

An underwater photograph taken by a bathyscope, of the wreck of the USS Thresher.

Air

The R.38 at Howden Aerodrome, just before setting off on her last flight.

The R.38: a minor setback

The R.38 was designed to be the greatest airship the world had known. It was larger than any built before, could cruise for 6500 miles and climb to an unprecedented height of 25,000 feet.

It was also ungainly and defective. The framework was too weak to support its weight and had to be strengthened to prevent buckling. But the R.38 was more than the largest airship that had been built. It was a project that involved the prestige of two nations: the British, whose Air Ministry had built it, and the American, who were buying it for use by their navy.

Before the Americans took over the ship, they insisted on some high speed tests. On 24 August 1921 the R.38 was on a trial flight with forty-nine British and American officers and men aboard. The ship had been in the air for thirty-five hours and had just completed a speed test, reaching sixty m.p.h. The commander reduced speed to forty-five m.p.h. and turned the R.38 sharply. Beneath him was the port of Hull, at its busiest at the end of a working day.

At that moment, the R.38 cracked open like an egg and fell in two halves. The wireless operator managed to send out the message: 'Ship broken, falling'. Fortunately for Hull, both parts of the ship fell into the river Humber. Four British and one American survived the crash.

The accident had no immediate impact on the many supporters of airships. They regarded it as a minor setback, the price that had to be paid for experimentation and progress. It did nothing to shake their faith in the superiority of the airship over the aircraft. It was obvious to them that the future lay with craft that were lighter than air.

As the American newspaper, the *New York World*, predicted with confidence: 'The theory of the dirigible remains so sound essentially that it will not be abandoned.'

It was to take another sixteen years and two terrible accidents to change people's minds.

The wreckage of the R.38.

The R.101: safe as houses

In any anthology of famous last words, a place would have to be found for the British Air Minister Lord Thompson's verdict on the airship R.101: 'She's as safe as a house, except for the millionth chance.' But he may not have been as convinced as he sounded: the day before he boarded the airship for its maiden flight to India he made his will.

As dusk fell on Saturday, 4 October 1930 the R.101 slipped its moorings and slowly, ponderously set off from Cardington into heavy rain. Lord Thompson and his retinue settled into the sybaritic routine that an airship provided. The wireless operator reported: 'After an excellent supper, our distinguished passengers smoked a final cigar and have now gone to bed.'

They passed London and made towards Paris. Over France, the weather grew more stormy and the R.101 began to lose height. It almost scraped the spire of the cathedral at Beauvais, a town some fifty miles from Paris.

Then, just outside the town, the airship suddenly dived low, hit a gently sloping hillside, and exploded into flames. There were only six survivors. Lord Thompson was killed with forty-seven others, victims of political expediency as much as of bad design.

For the R.101 had been a pet project of the Labour government then in power. They had also given a contract for the building of another airship, the R.100, to the engineering firm of Vickers. It was a deliberate competition, state control versus private enterprise, made bitter by the intense rivalry between the two teams.

Working on the R.101 were the men who had designed and built the ill-fated R.38. When it was built, the R.101 was so heavy that it could hardly rise off the ground. The designers' solution was to cut the ship in half and add a new forty-foot-long bay in the middle. They worked under considerable stress, for Lord Thompson had decided that he would fly to India in the R.101, and his schedule left no time for mistakes to be rectified.

When delays occurred, his reaction was: 'I must insist on the programme for the Indian flight being adhered to, as I have made my plans accordingly.' There was an Imperial Conference in London on 20 October. What better way to arrive there than having flown to Karachi and back?

Vickers' R.100 was a success, too, performing well on her trials, and making a faultless maiden flight to Canada. No one concerned with the R.101, and certainly not the Air Minister, wished to lose face. Lord Thompson is said to have expressed doubts about the airship privately, but he felt that it was his public duty to make the trip. He also expected to become the next Viceroy of India.

On a test flight on 20 June great tears appeared in the cover of the R.101. On 28 June, she flew at the Hendon Air Pageant, lurching ungracefully across the sky, almost impossible to control.

Time ran out for the designers and the crew. The R.101 left on her flight to India without a proper safety certificate of airworthiness, with trial flights incomplete, and with an exhausted crew who had hardly slept for three days while they prepared the ship for Lord Thompson. In other circumstances, it is doubtful whether the ship would have continued its journey into the worsening weather over France.

As the official inquiry under Sir John Simon reported: 'It is impossible to avoid the conclusion that R.101 would not have started for India on the evening of 4 October if it had not been that reasons of public policy were considered as making it highly desirable for her to do so.'

The inquiry, which predictably decided that no one was to blame, concluded that the main cause of the disaster was the loss of gas in bad weather. Some experts insisted that the crash came so quickly that it must have been due to the new bay breaking in two.

Two days after the crash, during an extraordinary séance, a well-known medium, Mrs Eileen Garrett, received messages, full of detailed technical information, purporting to come from the R.101's dead captain, who said that he knew the ship was faulty before the flight began.

Further speculation came from Neville Shute, the novelist who was deputy chief engineer on the rival R.100. Three weeks before the disaster, he had seen outer fabric of the R.101 that had disintegrated due to a chemical reaction to rubber adhesive. Perhaps some of the rotted fabric had not been replaced before the flight and had given way during the high winds?

It seems incredible now that men put such trust in such fragile, dangerous, and cumbersome objects as airships. Before the crash, there had been excited talk of linking

The tangled girders strewn on a French hillside were all that remained of the R.101.

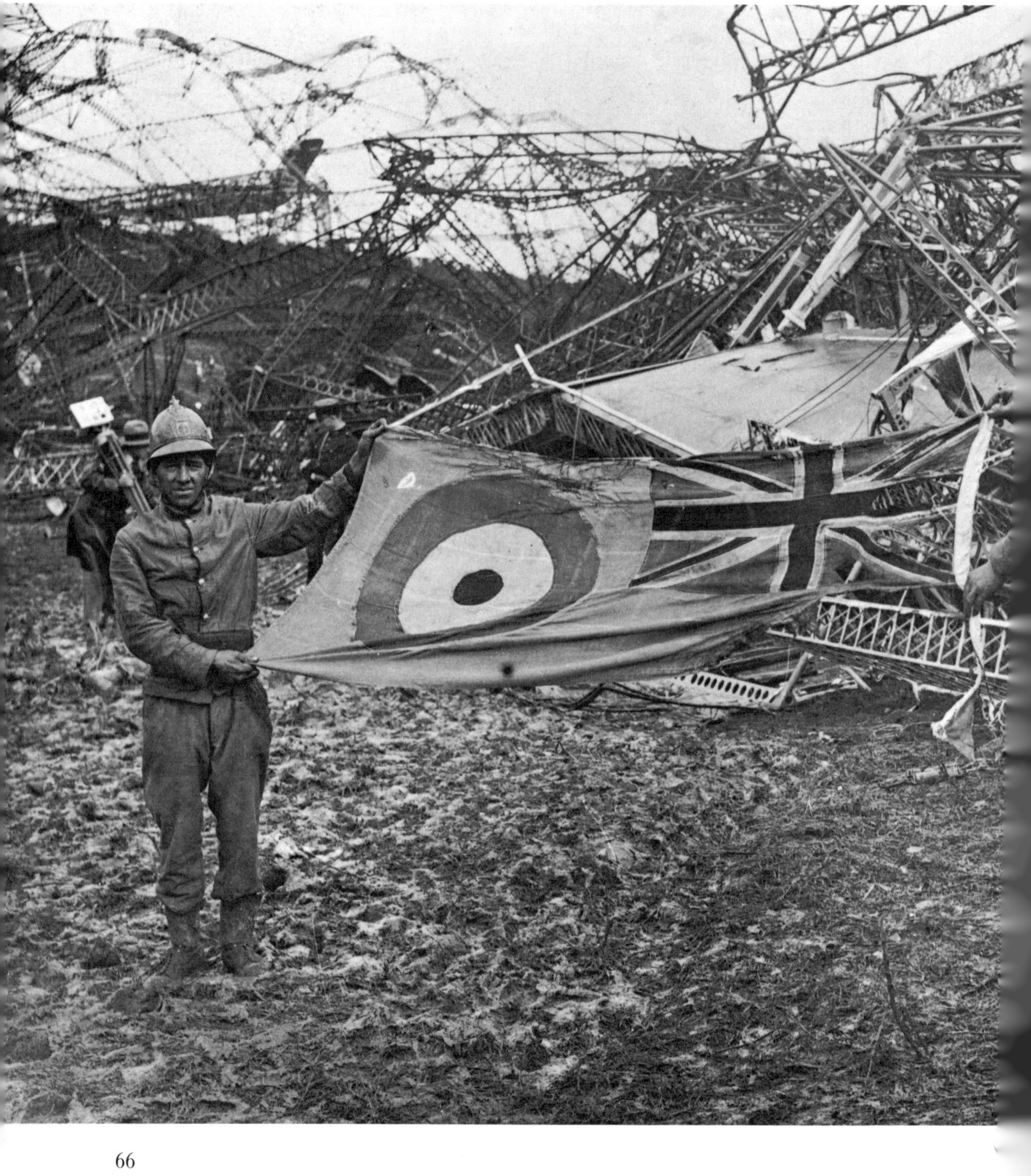

the British Empire by such ships, and forecasts of 1000-foot-long airships making regular transatlantic flights by the 1950s. Those hopes died, with the R.101, on the Beauvais hillside. Even the successful R.100 did not survive long after the crash. In 1931, it was scrapped.

French firemen hold aloft the tattered flag that survived the wreck of the R.101.

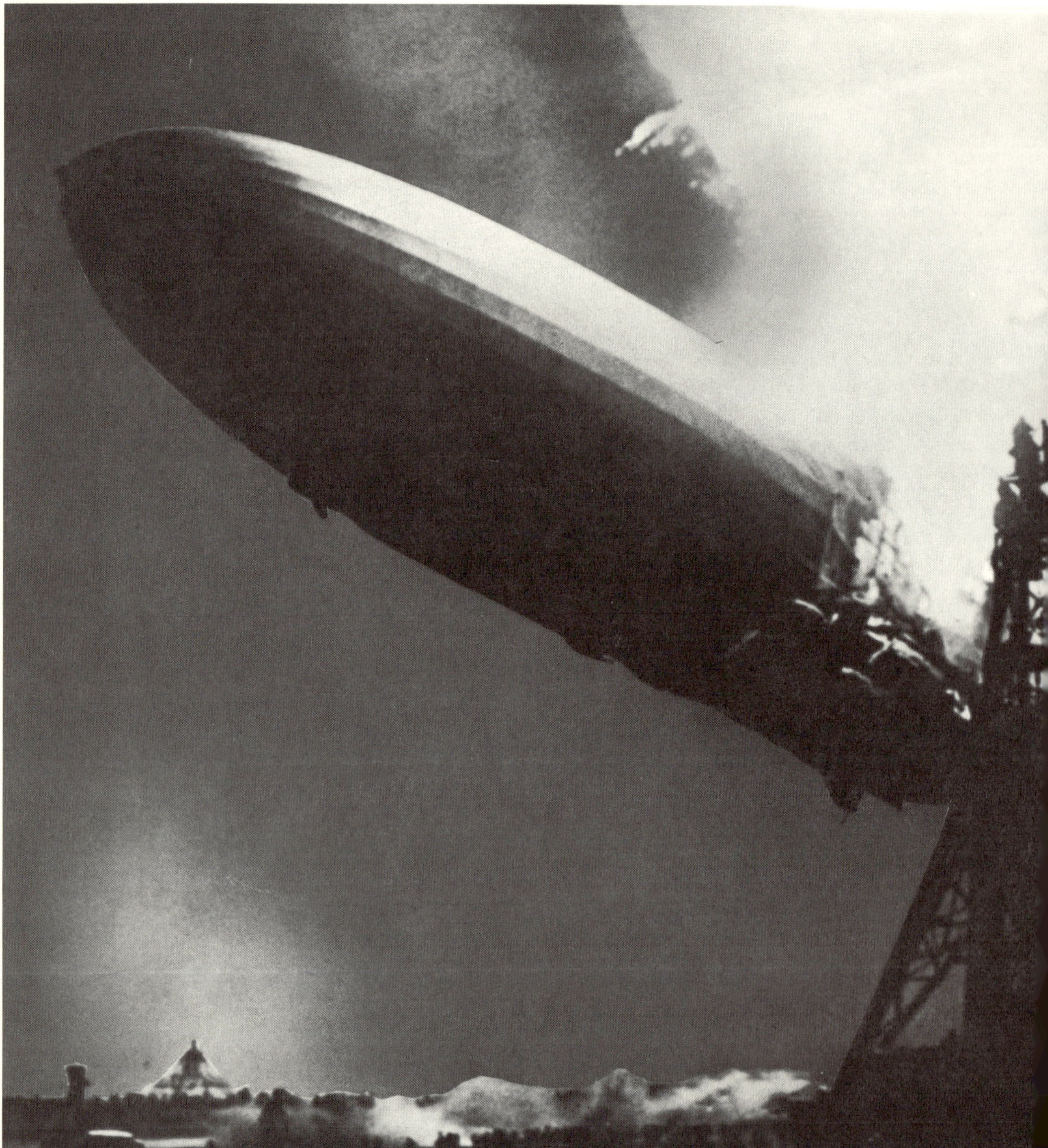

The Hindenburg: a mysterious spark

It has become one of the most famous of all radio commentaries:

'The Hindenburg is floating down like a feather, ladies and gentlemen', began Herbert Morrison, just before 7 p.m. on 11 May 1937 as the huge German airship, 830 feet long and 125 feet high, arrived at Lakehurst Naval Station, sixty miles from New York.

'The ropes have been dropped and they have been taken hold of by a number of men on the field', he continued casually, for he was recording for possible broadcast the next day, so routine was the occasion. 'The back motors of the ship are holding it just enough to keep it . . .' he said and paused. And went on in an anguished yell that broke into tears:

> It's broken into flames. It's flashing. It's flashing terribly! This is terrible! This is one of the worst catastrophes in the world. Oh! the humanity and all the passengers. I told you it's a mass of smoking wreckage. Honest, I can hardly breathe. Folks, I'm going to have to stop for a moment because I've lost my voice. This is the worst thing I've ever witnessed.

The flames, according to Morrison, were 500 feet in the sky. It took just thirty-two seconds for the Hindenburg to burn. Twenty of the crew, fifteen passengers, and one of the ground staff died. The cause of the sudden fire is still a mystery.

The evening was a stormy one and some, including the Hindenburg's commander, who briefly survived the accident, believe that it was struck by lightning or by St

The Hindenburg flashes into flames as it touches the mooring mast at Lakehurst Aerodrome.

69

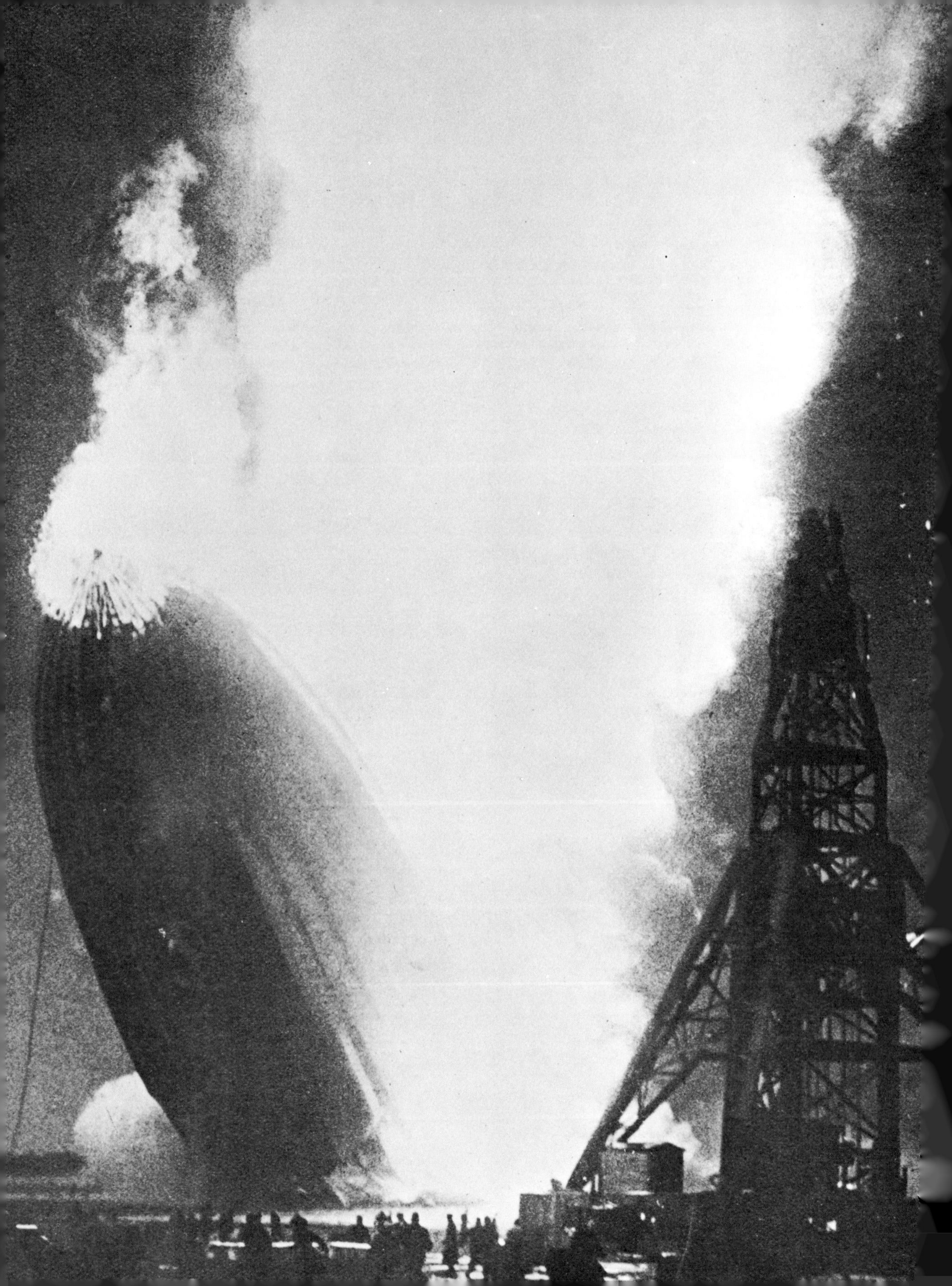

The Hindenburg falls to the ground in flames.

Elmo's Fire, a discharge of atmospheric electricity, as it came alongside the mooring mast. Sabotage was talked of, although an inquiry found no evidence to support this claim.

According to the latest theory, advanced by the American author Michael M. Mooney, the inquiry deliberately ignored the possibility of sabotage because they did not wish to cause an international incident. The German observers at the inquiry acquiesced in this out of pride. Mr Mooney claims that one of the crew, a twenty-five-year-old rigger, Eric Spehl, planted a phosphorous bomb aboard the ship that was timed to go off after everyone had disembarked. Because the Hindenburg was delayed in mooring by bad weather, the bomb exploded with passengers and crew still aboard. The reason for the sabotage was as a protest against the Nazi régime's persecution of Roman Catholic priests and nuns. The theory lacks the confirmation of Spehl himself, for he was fatally injured in the explosion.

Another explanation was advanced at the time by some of the ground crew. They claimed that one of the port engines was sparking. It is just conceivable that a spark could have been carried to the gas-release valves on the top of the ship's hull to set off the explosion.

Ironically, the Hindenburg had been designed to fly with helium, a non-inflammable gas, instead of the potentially dangerous hydrogen that was used. The disadvantage of helium was its cost of $10 (£3·80) per 1000 cubic feet—the Hindenburg required 6,750,000 cubic feet of gas—and the fact that America was its only source. Hitler's government decided that it would be wrong to waste reserves of foreign currency on helium, especially when hydrogen, much cheaper if inflammable, was easily available in Germany.

The City of Liverpool crash: sabotage or accident?

There was a feeling of shock in March 1933 over the mysterious crash of the luxury airliner the City of Liverpool. It was still the early days of civil aviation. Regular passenger flights had begun in Britain just fourteen years earlier. The accident, with its thirteen deaths, was the worst air disaster there had been. It still remains one of the most curious.

The 'plane had left Brussels for Croydon on the afternoon of 28 March. At 1.35 p.m., forty-nine minutes after take-off, Belgian farm workers saw it lose height as smoke and flames began to pour from its tail.

At the same moment, something fell from the aircraft, a small, dark object that twisted and turned in the air before it hit the ground. It was the body of one of the passengers, Albert Voss, a sixty-eight-year-old German who had become a naturalized Britain and

1

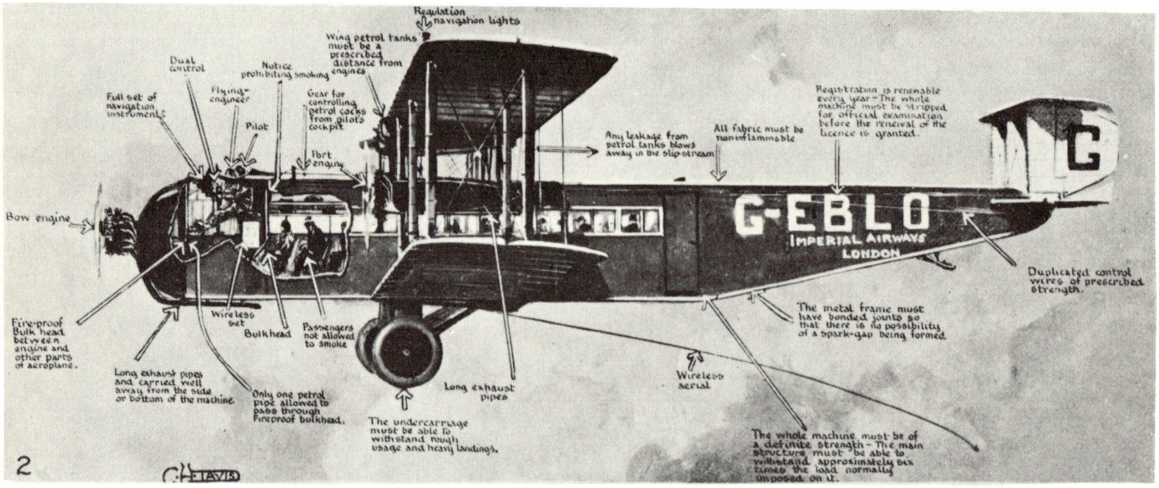
Regulation navigation lights
Wing petrol tanks must be a prescribed distance from engines
Dual control
Notice prohibiting smoking
Full set of navigation instruments
Flying-engineer
Pilot
Gear for controlling petrol cocks from pilot's cockpit
Port engine
Any leakage from petrol tanks blows away in the slip-stream
All fabric must be noninflammable
Registration is renewable every year - The whole machine must be stripped for official examination before the renewal of the licence is granted.
G
Bow engine
G-EBLO
IMPERIAL AIRWAYS
LONDON
Duplicated control wires of prescribed strength.
Fire-proof Bulk head between engine and other parts of aeroplane.
Wireless set
Bulkhead
Passengers not allowed to smoke
The metal frame must have bonded joints so that there is no possibility of a spark-gap being formed.
Long exhaust pipes and carried well away from the side or bottom of the machine.
Only one petrol pipe allowed to pass through Fireproof bulkhead.
Long exhaust pipes
Wireless aerial
The undercarriage must be able to withstand rough usage and heavy landings.
The whole machine must be of a definite strength - The main structure must be able to withstand approximately six times the load normally imposed on it.

2

worked in Manchester as a dentist and an importer of dental equipment.

Voss was an undischarged bankrupt who still managed to live well, a manic-depressive with suicidal tendencies, and had been investigated by both British and German police, although no charges had ever been brought against him. Before leaving Brussels, he insured himself against dying in an air accident for £500 ($1300). Aboard the 'plane, he sat at the rear, nearest the door.

As Voss's body fell from the City of Liverpool, and the 'plane continued to lose height, the pilot tried to guide it towards some open ground. No more than 200 feet from safety the 'plane split in half, the front section bursting into flames as it hit the ground.

Investigators into the crash decided that it was caused by a fire in the rear of the passenger cabin. There were two possible explanations: sabotage by means of a time-bomb; or accident, either through a misplaced cigarette end or some chemical cause.

Scotland Yard was called in, and detectives took away Voss's body a few days before the funeral. The circumstances, said the coroner at the inquest, were 'grave, suspicious'.

Had Voss committed a spectacular suicide and sabotage? Could he have caused the fire accidentally? The pathologist's report revealed that he died from multiple injuries from his fall.

The coroner told the jury at Voss's inquest:

You might think that the case is not entirely free from suspicion, but suspicion is not enough. In the absence of definite and direct evidence you would not be justified in saying that Voss was guilty of such a terrible crime. You will probably think that there is no evidence on which you can possibly return a verdict of suicide, and not sufficient evidence to show that he was in any way responsible for the fire.

The jury thought no such thing. They brought in an open verdict. Imperial Airways, who operated the 'plane as their luxury airliner, issued a statement saying that they had never suggested that Voss deliberately set fire to the City of Liverpool.

But, for the public, the case was proven. Voss's family found themselves the target of poison pen letters. Three months after the inquest, Albert Voss's widow died. Her body was found floating in the Manchester Ship Canal.

Top the City of Liverpool, an airliner of the Argosy class, a three-engined biplane. *Centre* a diagram showing the safety regulations of the time. *Bottom* the smouldering wreckage of the City of Liverpool.

The Munich crash: the day a football team died

Their names formed a litany that could be chanted by anyone in Britain who thought of himself as a soccer enthusiast: Roger Byrne, Geoff Bent, Bobby Charlton, Duncan Edwards, Jackie Pegg, Tommy Taylor, Billy Whelan . . .

They were members of Manchester United's football team, managed by the tough Matt Busby and dubbed 'Busby's Babes' by the press, for the average age of the team was not much over twenty. They were not only a young team, but one of the finest ever assembled. They had been league champions in Britain for two consecutive years and looked as if they might remain on top for a third year. The year before, they had come close to winning the F.A. Cup Final, only losing after their goalkeeper was carried off the field, and they had reached the European Cup final, which they lost to Real Madrid.

Now, in February 1958, they had reached the semi-finals of the European Cup, drawing 3-3 with Red Star of Belgrade, after Bobby Charlton had scored two goals. They had won the first leg of the two matches 2-1 to give them a win on aggregate.

The jubilant team, with their manager and club officials—a party of twenty-one altogether—and with eleven British sports journalists and photographers boarded in Belgrade a BEA twin-engined Elizabethan, which they had chartered as they needed to return quickly to Britain for an important league game. There were six other passengers.

The first part of the flight went smoothly. Then they landed at Munich to refuel. That did not take very long. But, as the plane accelerated along the runway for take-off, the pilot abruptly abandoned his attempt. He taxied back and tried again. Again he stopped. He was worried by the sudden variations in the petrol pressure indicator. This time, he went to fetch an engineer and the passengers returned to wait in the airport.

It was not long before they again embarked. The engineer had explained that the variations were due to the altitude of Munich airport. But, by now, the plane had been waiting for 106 minutes. The weather was freezing cold, and it was snowing.

On the third attempt at take-off, as the Elizabethan neared the end of the runway, its speed, then 117 knots, suddenly dropped. It would not accelerate. By now, it was too late for the pilot to pull up. The plane left the runway, heading straight for a house that stood 300 yards further on. Its port wing smashed into the building. The plane veered to the right, hit a hut, broke into pieces and caught fire. Two footballers, Bobby Charlton and Dennis Violett, were thrown clear by the impact and escaped without serious injury.

But some of their colleagues—Roger Byrne, the team captain, Geoff Bent, Eddie Colman, David Pegg, Mark Jones, Tommy Taylor, Billy Whelan—died instantly, as did eight journalists. Others, including the pilot and Duncan Edwards, regarded by many as one of the finest players in the world, died later in hospital. Others recovered, including the team manager Matt Busby, whose condition was at first so serious that the last rites were administered to him. In all, twenty-three died.

Had the house not been where it was, so near the runway, it is possible that the accident might have been a minor one, with injuries no worse than cuts or bruises. But its position broke neither the German nor the international air regulations.

An inquiry in Germany decided that ice on the wing had contributed to the disaster. During the plane's wait at the airport, a layer of frozen snow had built up on the

Part of the wreckage of the crashed Manchester United plane.

wing, affecting the aircraft's aerodynamic qualities. It was impossible to determine what other causes there were for the crash.

It was the worst disaster in British sporting history. Amazingly, Manchester United, with a team made up mainly of reserves, went on to win their next game, an F.A. Cup match against Sheffield Wednesday. And, while they lost many League games, spurred on by their supporters, they once again reached the F.A. Cup Final at Wembley, only to lose there 2–0 to Bolton.

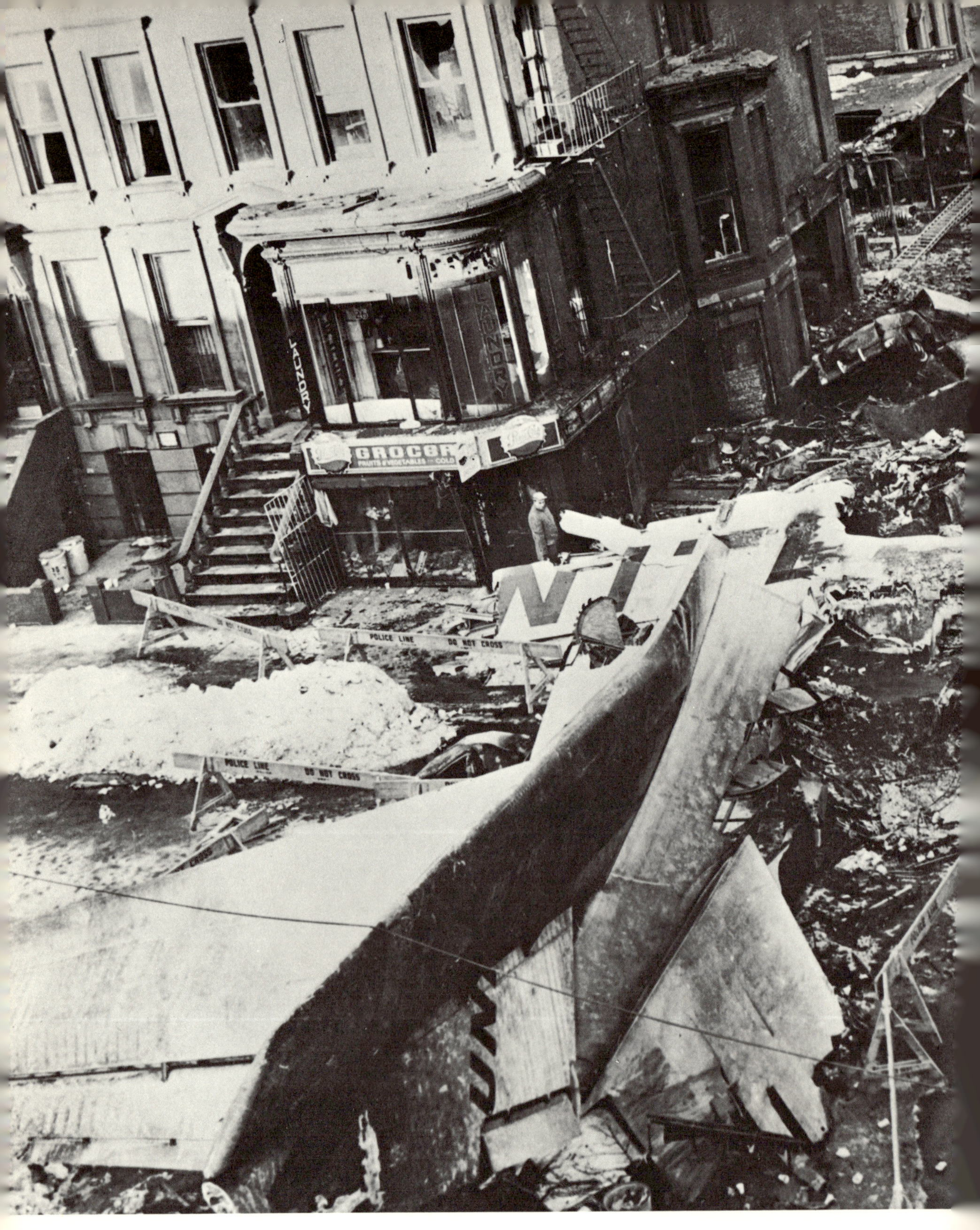

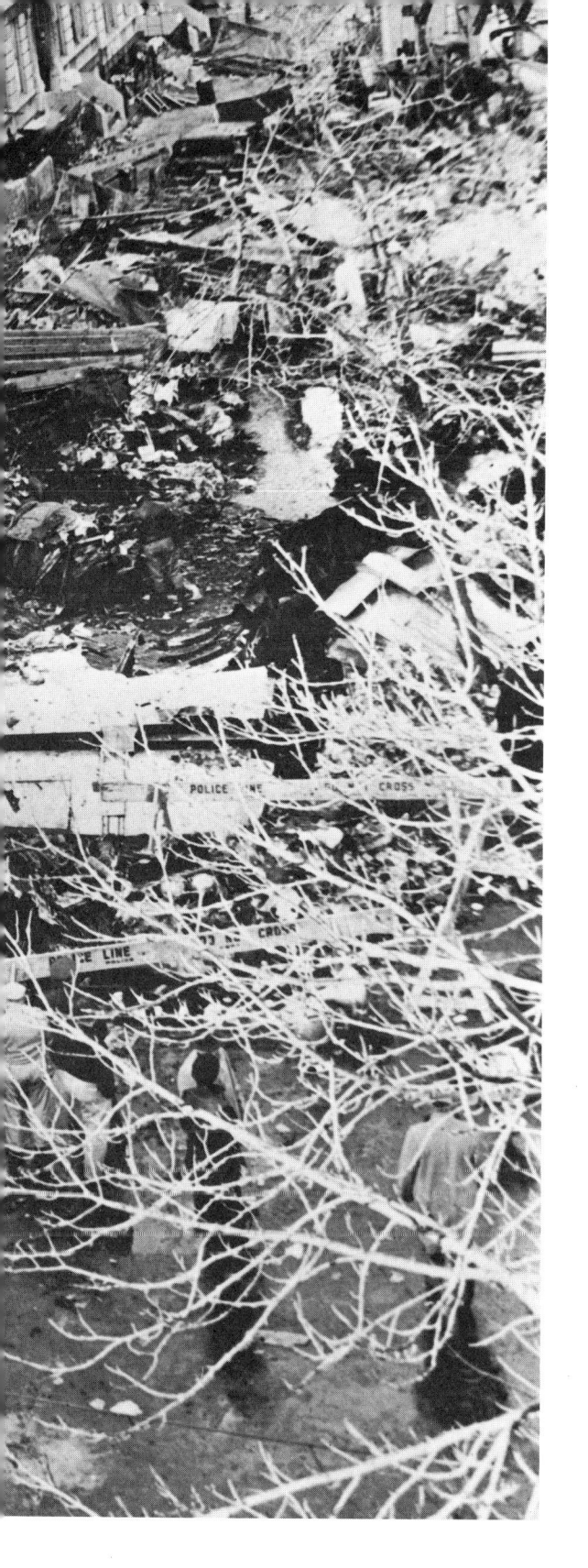

The Staten Island crash: a mid-air meeting

On Friday, 16 December 1960 a United Airlines DC-8 jet, carrying seventy-seven passengers and a crew of seven, was approaching Idlewild Airport after a flight from Chicago. A Trans World Airlines four-engined Constellation, with thirty-nine passengers and four crew aboard, was heading for La Guardia Airport from Ohio.

As their journeys neared their end, in a snowstorm over New York, the two 'planes collided. The DC-8 fell in flames on to a tenement district of Brooklyn, shattering buildings and setting shops aflame, among them a chapel belonging to the Pillar of Fire church. There was one survivor from the 'plane, and eight others died on the ground.

The Constellation fell into the harbour by Staten Island, across New York Bay from Brooklyn, wrecking a few houses. There were no survivors. The death toll of 135 was the worst mid-air collision up to that date. It could have been worse: the DC-8 narrowly missed a school containing 1700 children.

The only person who briefly survived the crash was an eleven-year-old boy. Before he died the next day from his injuries, he described what had happened:

> I remember looking out of the 'plane window at the snow below covering the city. It looked like a picture out of a fairy book. It was a beautiful sight. Then, suddenly there was an explosion. The 'plane started to fall and people started to scream. I held on to my seat and then the 'plane crashed. That's all I remember.

Police blockades mark out the area of Brooklyn damaged by the crashing DC-8 jet airliner. The tail section demolished a funeral home that stood on the street corner.

The Maracaibo crash: death on the ground

Within two minutes of taking off from the Grano De Oro Airport at Maracaibo, Venezuela, a DC-9 jet, which had been in service for ten days, lost altitude, hit a high tension wire, and crashed and exploded on to a housing estate.

There were no survivors among the eighty-four people aboard the jet, operated by Viasa, the Venezuelan national airline. Blazing fuel from the 'plane set alight cars, trucks, and houses in La Trinidad, a new housing estate that formed a suburb of Ziruna.

Another seventy-one people died on the ground. Police found the bodies of a mother and her children, killed at their meal, and two dead children clutching the body of a dog.

The crash of 16 March, 1969 has never been satisfactorily explained. It was almost a brand-new 'plane, and the weather was perfect. Some eyewitnesses claimed that the jet's port engine caught fire as it took off. Sabotage was suspected, but nothing has ever been proved.

The Shizukuishi collision: out of a clear blue sky

Sergeant Yoshimi Ichikawa, a twenty-two-year-old with twenty-one hours' flying experience, was at the controls of a Sabre jet fighter flying in the clear blue summer sky 27,000 feet above the Japanese town of Shizukuishi. Suddenly the voice of his instructor cut in from another jet nearby: 'Pull up! Right turn!'

The warning came too late. Ichikawa's jet collided with an All-Nippon Airways Boeing 727 carrying 162 people, many of them on a package tour organized by the Bereaved Family Association for the relatives of men who had died in World War II. The Boeing disintegrated and caught fire, scattering wreckage and bodies on the paddy fields beneath. Ichikawa, who was flying on a simulated interceptor training mission, parachuted to safety.

All those aboard the Boeing died, a disaster that surpassed all others in the history of aviation. In the angry aftermath, some politicians claimed that Japan's Self Defence Force used civil airliners for target practice, and the director-general of the government's Defence Agency resigned. He was criticized for standing upright and wearing shoes while apologizing to the relatives of the dead. According to custom, he should have been barefoot and kneeling. The Japanese Prime Minister added his 'bitter regrets' in an apology to the nation.

The disaster emphasized a situation that exists in every country in the world—namely, that the sky is overcrowded. Accidents, too, involve more casualties as 'planes grow larger. The first jumbo jet crash could kill as many as 500 people, and airlines are already talking of 'planes that will carry 1000 passengers.

There is also increasing competition for air space between civil and military aircraft. Near collisions in the sky are an increasingly common occurrence. In Japan, it was estimated that 377 near-misses between military and other aircraft had happened over a period of five years.

In 1971 the British Airline Pilots Association expressed concern at the figures of recorded near-misses for 1970. The number, eleven, was three times as high as in the previous year. They also complained that fighter aircraft were using civil airliners for target practice over Europe.

In 1969, the International Air Transport Association recorded 290 near-misses over France, Germany, Spain, Switzerland, Italy, the Netherlands, and Britain. 36.9 per cent of them happened over Germany, and 22.7 per cent over France.

Until the Shizukuishi crash on Friday, 30 July 1971, the highest number of passengers to be killed in an air accident was 133. They died on 4 February 1966 when an All-Nippon Airways Boeing 727 crashed into Tokyo Bay while approaching the airport. (Coincidentally, a month later a Canadian DC-8 crash-landed at Tokyo airport killing sixty-four people. And just eighteen hours after that a BOAC Boeing 707 crashed in flames at the foot of Mount Fuji, fifty miles from Tokyo, killing 124.)

The worst American aircraft disaster involving a single 'plane came on 4 September 1971 when an Alaska Airlines Boeing 727 crashed into a 2500-foot-high mountainside in the Tongass National Forest, Alaska, killing 104 passengers and the crew of seven.

The Apollo fire: complacency and competitiveness

Colonel Virgil Grissom, the first American to make two space flights, Lieutenant-Colonel Edward White, the first American to walk in space, and Lieutenant-Commander Roger Chaffee were the team chosen to make the first manned flight in an Apollo spacecraft.

Blast-off was fixed for 27 February 1967. On 27 January, during the first of a series of tests on the launch-pad at Cape Kennedy, they entered the craft at 3 p.m. for a simulated lift-off at 6.41 p.m. But their final countdown went:

6.31.03 p.m. Chaffee reports a fire in the spacecraft.
6.31.04. According to the indication of the control system, the crew begin to move inside the craft. Probably White was reaching over his shoulder for the inner release handle of the hatch, the beginning of the emergency escape drill.
6.31.05. The temperature inside the cabin starts to rise.
6.31.09. White's voice is heard, confirming that there is a fire. As the pressure in the cabin begins to rise because of the heat, there is more movement. Probably Grissom was helping White in the next step of the escape procedure.
6.31.12. The cabin temperature rises rapidly. Chaffee is heard again, saying that a bad fire exists. He turns on the craft's internal batteries and increases the

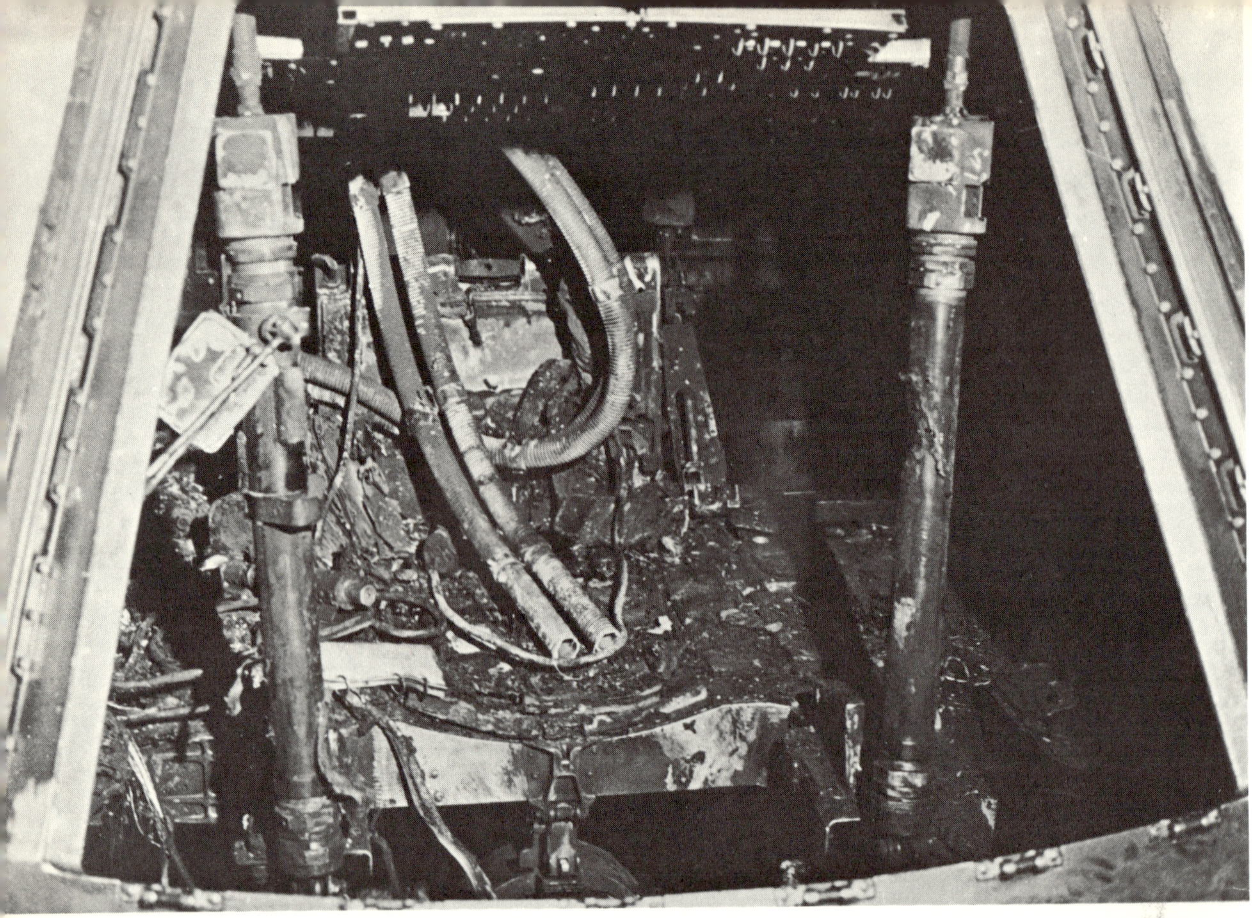

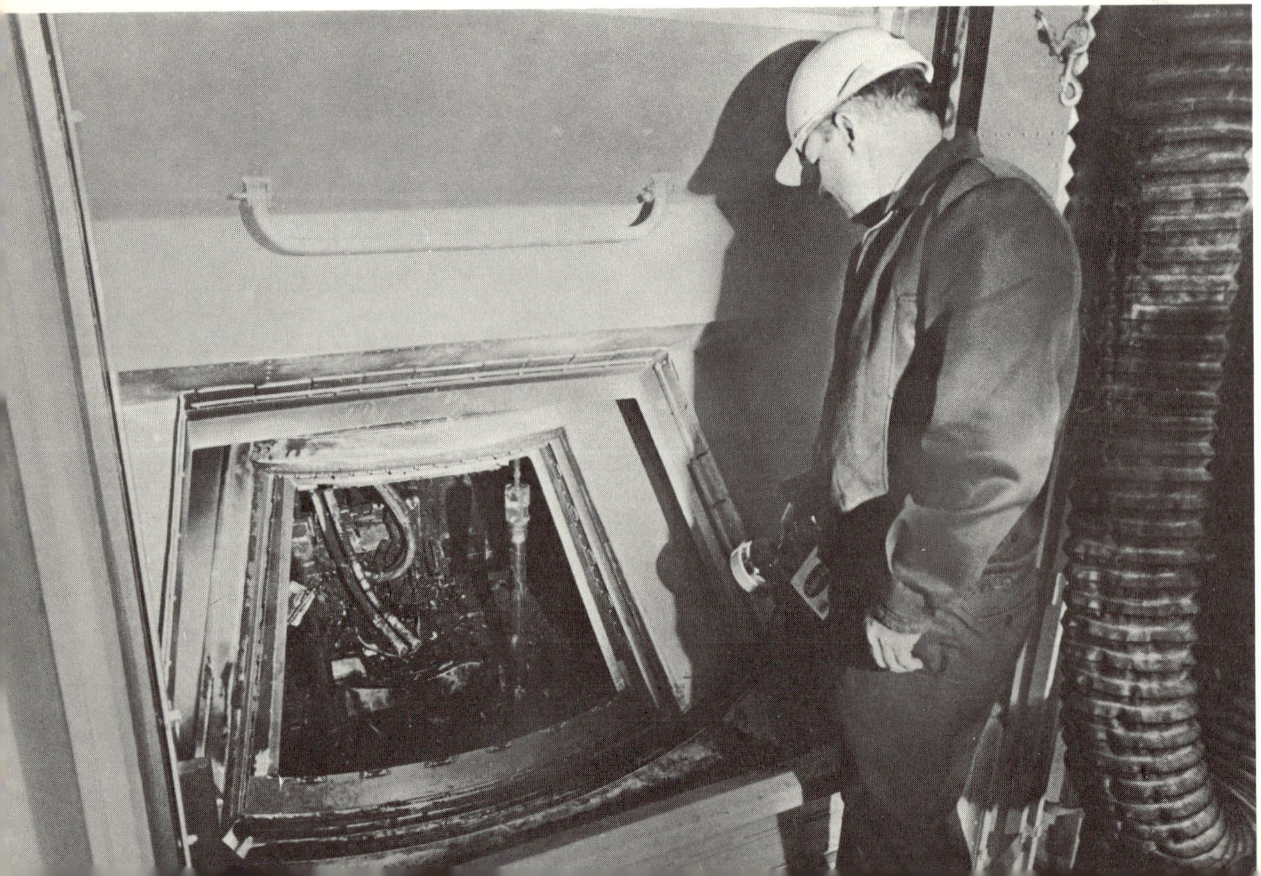

Above
The interior of the Apollo spacecraft, after the fire.
Below
A close-up of the burned-out space capsule in which three astronauts died.

illumination of the cabin lights.

6.31.17. As the pressure inside the cabin reaches 29 lb. per square inch, the capsule bursts. Said the official report: 'Some listeners believe that there was one sharp cry of pain.' Rescuers found the bodies of the three men in a heap at the entrance to the hatch.

The fire that killed them began in a bundle of wiring beneath a small equipment access door in the cabin. Conditions were ideal for a fierce fire: the sealed cabin was pressurized with pure oxygen; the plumbing contained a corrosive and combustible coolant which caught fire when soldered joints melted in the heat; there was plenty of inflammable material in the cabin, including a nylon net slung to stop objects floating or falling into the complicated equipment, and the insulation of the breathing control unit and the adhesive pads to which astronauts attached equipment.

The official inquiry found many deficiencies in the Apollo's design, engineering, manufacture, and quality control. A wrench socket, for instance, had been left between two bundles of wiring.

It also condemned the inadequate provisions for the crew to escape and the slowness of the rescue attempts. Because the Apollo team devoted its effort to solving the many complex problems of space travel, they failed to give adequate attention to mundane but equally vital questions of crew safety.

Another reason was complacency, for men had been put into orbit sixteen times in six years without mishap. Then, too, there was the competitiveness of space exploration, the American desire to stay ahead of the Russians, so that risks—perhaps unjustifiable ones—were judged acceptable and necessary.

The Soyuz II leak: payment of an unfair price

In a rhetorical tribute to his fellow cosmonauts, the Russian Vladislav Volkov, an author as well as an engineer, wrote:

> Must man have courage to dare? Certainly! And risky thoughts? And labour? At times the most difficult labour when the day seems not to have twenty-four hours but only two-and-a-half? And risk? Risk, passing into daring, to the very last boundary, when suddenly you realize with utter clarity that you cannot bear the load.
>
> Not because your strength is inadequate but because you will not have the time; you will simply not have the time to finish. Your stellar hours are not perpetual motion; they will stop. Some time,

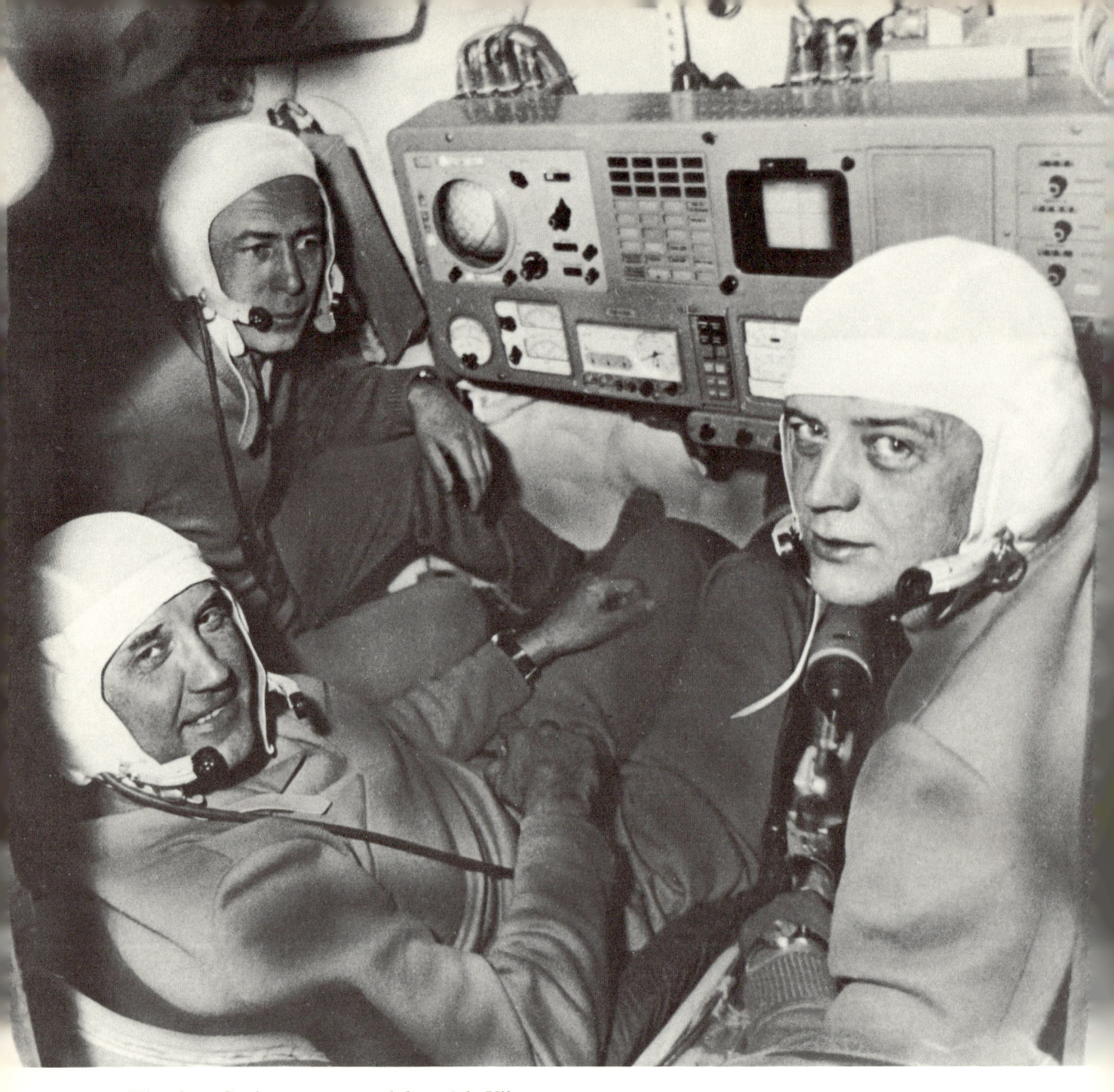

The three Soviet cosmonauts *left to right* Viktor Patsayev, Georgi Dobrovolsky, and Vladislav Volkov, in the cabin of Soyuz II.

unfortunately, they must stop, the hours of your life.

A few days after correcting the proofs of the book in which these words appear, time stopped for Volkov and his two companions, Georgi Dobrovolsky and Viktor Patsayev. On 30 June 1971 they crossed that last boundary as their spacecraft, Soyuz II, re-entered the earth's atmosphere after a flight lasting twenty-three days, seventeen hours, and forty-one minutes, over six days longer than any of man's previous journeys into space.

Until that final moment, thirty minutes before their craft made a successful landing in the steppes of Kazakhstan, their mission had been a success. They had docked their spacecraft with the orbiting space station Salyut, a manoeuvre that proved it was possible to supply an unmanned space laboratory with crews from earth.

Aboard the Salyut, they had carried out a series of scientific experiments. Patsayev had celebrated his thirty-eighth birthday there, with presents of an onion and a lemon that his colleagues had smuggled aboard.

The three, the first men to die in space, were found still strapped in their seats by the engineers who opened the hatch of their capsule. Their bodies lay in state in the Central House of the Soviet Army before they were cremated and their remains placed in the Kremlin wall.

An inquiry reported that death was caused by a rapid drop in pressure during the descent of the Soyuz, due to a loss of the ship's sealing. But there was no explanation of what caused the loss although, in Moscow, many claimed that the crew had not closed their hatch properly. During the turbulence of re-entry, the hatch opened slightly and the oxygen was sucked out, it was claimed.

Whatever the cause, the cosmonauts would have died within fifteen seconds as their blood boiled off in the sudden vacuum. As the Soviet poet Yevgeny Yevtushenko said: 'The price they had to pay was not fair.'

But what their deaths revealed was man's

A drawing of the Soyuz II just before docking with the space station Salyut, where the cosmonauts carried out experiments.

Leaders of the Soviet Government and Communist Party *left to right* K. Mazurov, A. Kirilenko, N. Podgorny, A. Kosygin, and L. Brezhnev, form a guard of honour at the cosmonauts' lying-in-state.

ignorance about the effects and dangers of prolonged space travel. What evidence there is suggests that weightlessness causes grave problems.

One of the side-effects of lack of gravity is a slowing of the heart-rate and a reduction in the amount of blood circulating in the body. When a cosmonaut re-enters the earth's atmosphere, his heart has to withstand great stress. The Russians who crewed Soyuz 9 were unable to walk for several days after their return because of the reaction of their bodies to conditions of gravity.

Space travellers have not only suffered from abnormal heart rhythms, but also from a loss of potassium in the blood stream, which reduces muscle tone, and a lowering of calcium in the bones, which become more brittle.

During a long stay in space, a cosmonaut's responses slow and he becomes less efficient in his work. Could the three Russians, in space longer than any before them, have become careless at the last? Towards the end of their mission they were tiring and, a couple of days before their return, Lieutenant-Colonel Dobrovolsky, the forty-three-year-old commander of the flight, radioed: 'We have had enough', an echo of Volkov's words: 'you realize with utter clarity that you cannot bear the load'.

Or were their deaths due not so much to mechanical or physiological failures as to some psychological fault? So far, no one has paid much attention to the psychological effects of space travel, even though American astronauts have reported feelings of severe depression following their return to earth. We do know that pilots flying at high altitudes sometimes make mistakes due to psychological factors.

Are cosmonauts likely to be any different? In our rush to explore outer space, are we overlooking the fact that we are also journeying into inner space, the dark and uncharted regions of our minds?

3 All fall down: bridge and dam disasters

The Coblenz footbridge collapse: a weighty occasion

There had never been so many people crowded into the streets of Coblenz as there were on 22 July 1930 to see the arrival of President von Hindenburg, then engaged on a triumphal tour of formerly occupied territory of the Rhineland. The city was packed almost to suffocation point.

One of its architectural splendours, the fortress of Ehrenbreistein, standing at the junction of the Rhine and the Moselle, was floodlit for the occasion. On the evening of the president's visit, the crowds were out in enormous numbers.

More than a hundred managed to clamber on a narrow wooden footbridge that joined the Moselle to a shipping basin. It provided a splendid view of the river scene, with the illuminated castle in the background.

As their enthusiasm reached its peak, the bridge collapsed under the weight of the people, throwing them into the river. It was dark and the current was swift. In the confusion, forty people drowned. The next day, Hindenburg cancelled his tour and returned to Berlin. As Coblenz's burgomaster said, the worst disaster in the city's history had come on its day of greatest rejoicing.

A search for bodies goes on after the collapse of a bridge across the Rhine at Coblenz.

The Quebec bridge collapse: an insufficiency of data

For years there had been talk of building a bridge across the St Lawrence river below Montreal, to replace the summer ferry and the winter's walk across the frozen waters. In 1904, work began on what was designed to be the greatest suspension bridge in the world, costing some $3,000,000 (£1,170,000). The bridge, with its approaches, was to be 3240 feet long with a main span of 1800 feet soaring 160 feet above the river.

There were problems during construction. The consulting engineer was not only old, over seventy, but also infirm so that he rarely left his home in New York. He was paid an inadequate salary, and could hardly afford to hire assistants, for the company provided him with none of the necessary staff.

On Friday, 29 August 1906, there were ninety-two construction workers on the bridge, preparing to finish for the day. It was 5.47 p.m. On the south side, a locomotive pulling three cars loaded with iron puffed out on to the partly built bridge.

As it did so, the anchor pier on the south side gave way, toppling into the river 800 feet of the steel superstructure. Eight of the men were picked up immediately by boats. Most of the others were trapped in the wreckage.

It was dark, and the rescuers had little light to guide them. Although they could hear the groans of men trapped, there was nothing they could do to extricate them. Soon the tide rose and drowned many of those pinned under the debris. The total of seventy dead included about thirty Caughnawaga Indians, a remnant of the Iroquois nation, as well as some American workers.

The collapse was caused by the failure of the lower chords in the anchor arm of the main pier, a failure not due to the materials used, but to the design. The chords gave way under stresses that were in no way exceptional.

The royal commission that investigated the collapse reported: 'No one connected with the general designing fully appreciated the magnitude of the work nor the insufficiency of the data upon which they were depending.'

And upon which the bridge gave way.

The Silver Bridge collapse: one out of nearly 90,000

The Christmas shopping rush was at its height and traffic was packed bumper to bumper across the steel and aluminium Silver Bridge spanning the Ohio River at Point Pleasant, West Virginia, when, without warning, it collapsed.

Some seventy-five cars and lorries were hurled down 120 feet into the fast flowing, seventy-foot-deep ice-cold water as the bridge, a quarter of a mile long, toppled,

The tangled wreckage of cars and trucks after the collapse of the Silver Bridge, Ohio.

leaving only the supporting piers visible. At least sixty vehicles were trapped under the water by the debris.

A few drivers managed to cling to the wreckage, but most were swept away. Forty-six died, nine were injured, and eighteen rescued alive. It happened on 15 December 1967. The bridge had been built nearly forty years before, in 1928. Twice in its last eighteen months of existence, state authorities had repaired it after local officials had pointed out weak spots. Two years earlier, a 'detailed' examination of the bridge had revealed no defects.

The seriousness of the situation was only realized when the Federal Highway Administration investigated the condition of some other of America's 563,000 bridges. In 1971, they estimated that 88,900 highway bridges were in a critically deficient state.

This total included several very long-span bridges whose collapse could cause a calamity exceeding the scale of the Silver Bridge disaster.

More than 400,000 of the bridges were built before 1935. Of the deficient bridges, 24,000 were on the federal-aid highway system. In 1971, the administration reckoned that it had enough funds to replace only fifty of the most dangerous. At that rate, it will be 480 years before America's bridges can be considered safe.

Yarra and Coblenz: the box girder failures

'The events which led to the disaster moved with the inevitability of a Greek tragedy', stated the Royal Commission that investigated what happened on 15 October 1970 when one of the largest bridges in the world, being built across the River Yarra, near Melbourne, Australia, collapsed, killing thirty-five workmen.

'That it should have been allowed to happen was inexcusable,' reported the Commission. 'There was no sudden onslaught of natural forces, no unexpected failure of new or untested material.'

But the Yarra Bridge was of experimental design, using the box girder method of construction. Box girder bridges have provided the most spectacular engineering failures of the century. They include the Danube bridge in Vienna, which collapsed in 1969, as well as the Milford Haven bridge which fell down in June 1970, killing five of the British workmen.

Those who are not engineers can derive some consolation from the fact that these bridges failed during construction so that the public was not exposed to danger.

The advantage of the box girder system is simply that it cuts the cost of bridge-building. Instead of the conventional methods of building a bridge, prefabricated units of steel boxes are slid out and welded or bolted to each other. This means that the boxes are under considerable strain until the next supporting pier is reached. At Yarra, the strain was too much.

'To a greater or lesser degree the river authority, the designers, the contractors, and even the labour engaged in the work must all take some part of the blame,' said the official inquiry.

On the site, there was animosity between the English and the Australian engineers, and the workers threatened to strike. 'Morale was bad and the direction and organization was largely ineffective,' said the inquiry.

The failure happened between piers 10 and 11 on the west side of the bridge, where the two box girders forming the span between the piers were found to be not level. There was a four-and-a-half inch gap between them. Ten eight-ton concrete blocks were placed on one section to force it into line with the other.

One of the sections also developed a buckle and a series of bolts was removed to alter the stresses and, it was hoped, straighten it out. At 8.30 a.m. on 15 October, as workmen removed the bolts, the buckle suddenly spread across the whole section.

Something had gone wrong, but no one seemed to know quite what. Quickly, the men were ordered to put back the bolts and

An aerial view of the bridge over the Yarra
River, showing the collapsed section.

others were sent to help them. The English engineer in charge, who had previously tried to resign from his job, telephoned the original Australian contractors for advice.

'Shall I get the bods off?' he asked, although he did not sound worried. Then he returned to the bridge. As he did so, the 367-foot-long span gave way, sending the concrete blocks crashing down to crush workmen's huts beneath. He was among those who died.

In the aftermath of the disaster, forty-two British road bridges, of steel box girder construction, were examined and traffic using them was restricted. Among the bridges that fell short of the government's safety standards was the Tinsley Viaduct, a mile-long bridge that forms part of the much-used M1 motorway.

The box girder experiment continued to go wrong. On Wednesday, 10 November 1971 a road bridge being built over the river Rhine at Coblenz collapsed, killing nine. In a previous bridge disaster at Coblenz, in 1930 (see page 86), forty people had drowned in the Rhine.

The Coblenz bridge was neither so light nor so cheap as its British counterparts. A prefabricated section of the bridge, weighing eighty-five tons, was being hoisted into place for welding by means of a crane standing on the end of the projecting span of the bridge.

With a noise like that of a sonic boom, the span, 189 feet long, jack-knifed and collapsed slowly into the river. The crane fell from the edge of the bridge on to a tug beneath, which had towed the box into place, killing the captain and eight workers.

Engineers have acknowledged that it is difficult to calculate the correct safety factor for box girder bridges, since it is exceedingly complex to work out how the boxes support each other and at what point they are likely to fail. The method has speed and cheapness to recommend it, even though that is being paid for by death and destruction. In commercial ventures, where does the responsibility of the engineer lie?

'Engineers do not know everything,' said Sir Hubert Shirley Smith, a member of the Royal Commission investigating the Yarra bridge collapse, as he questioned a witness.

'They cannot pretend they know everything and the sooner they admit they do not know everything, the better. We must make adequate allowance for the factor of ignorance.

'Do you agree?'

The Vaiont Dam disaster: a slip between the basin and the lip

The Vaiont Dam, in the Piave Valley, is one of the greatest feats of Italian engineering. More than 870 feet high, it is the third highest concrete dam in the world, providing hydro-electric power for the region and forming a huge reservoir that laps the edge of Mount Toc, a bare expanse of rock some 6000 feet high.

The dam was finished in 1960. By 1963, some of the engineers were becoming a little worried about the mountain. Little vegetation grew on it so that there was nothing to bind together the earth and rock and provide some stability. And there was a distressing

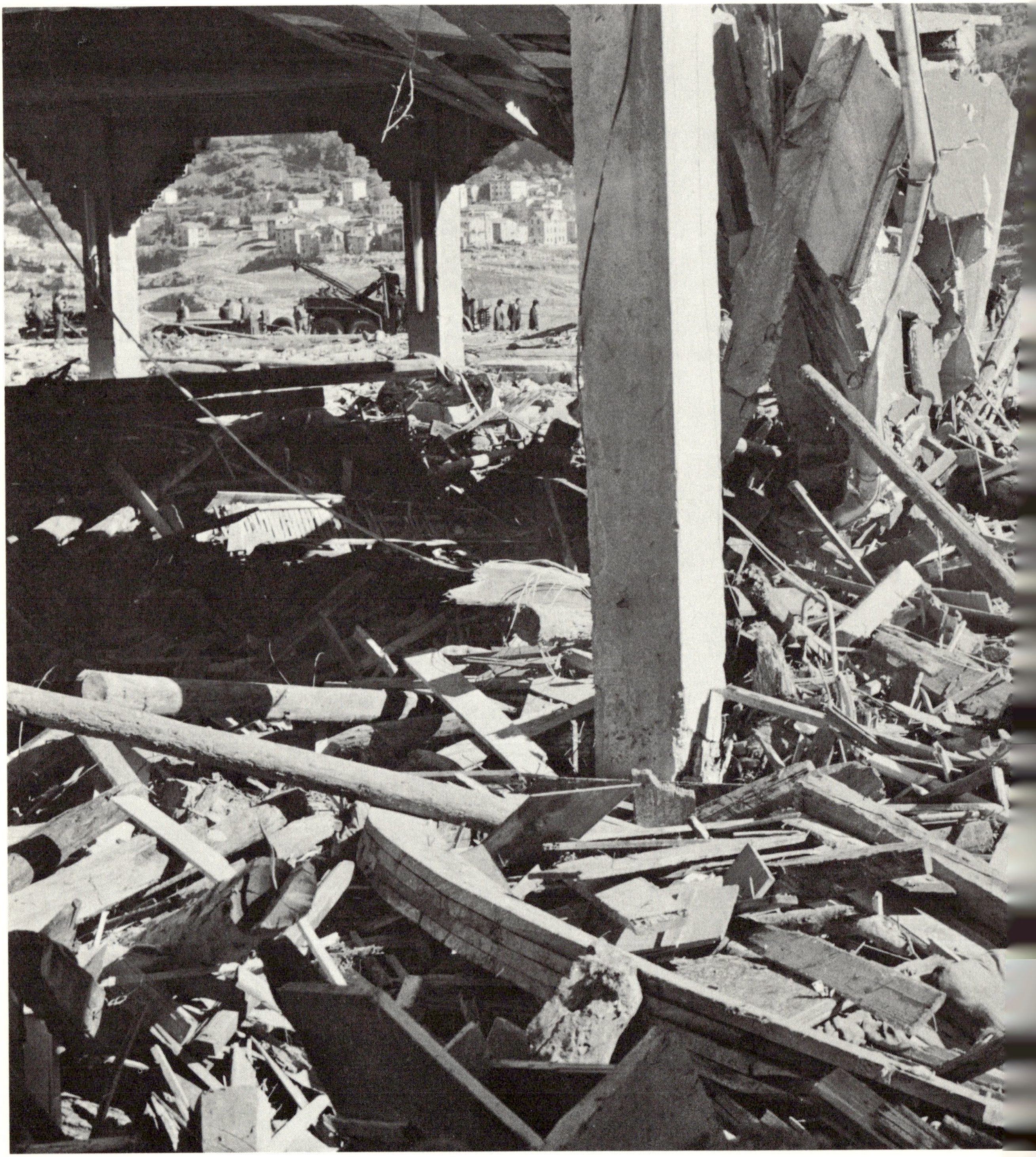

tendency for the mountainside to slide, little by little, into the basin of the dam.

Below the dam, the people who lived in small scattered communities regarded it with some fear. In the largest village, Longarone, where 2000 lived, the inhabitants used to joke about it, as if a shrug and a smile were enough to appease the danger they felt.

That October, 1963, was a wet one, with torrential rain lashing against the mountainside. After a further stormy day, at 11 p.m. on Wednesday, 9 October the rockface of Mount Toc, loosened by the rain, slipped violently, sending half the mountainside, 260,000,000 cubic metres of earth and rock, crashing down into the basin of the dam at a speed of thirty m.p.h.

The sudden, enormous slide sent a huge wave speeding across the basin and over the lip of the dam to cascade on the villages beneath. A wall of water 600 feet high rushed across the valley, totally submerging the village of Longarone and the surrounding countryside, flattening houses and buildings and creating a wasteland of mud and stones.

The road and railway lines to Longarone were washed away for a mile. At first, the only survivors were thought to be seven people who had managed to outrun the water and reach some high ground before the wave overwhelmed the village. Six other communities were also washed out. The valley, said an eye-witness, looked like Pompeii before the excavations were begun.

It was difficult to establish the numbers of the dead, since municipal records were destroyed and tiny communities wholly disappeared. The final official figure was 1899 dead, including 311 children under ten years of age. Six days later, the mountain slid again and villages had to be evacuated. In one village, sixteen people were injured in a panic that followed a rumour that the dam had given way.

The disaster was not so natural as it

Ruins of a church in the town of Longarone, devastated by the breaking of the Vaiont dam.

A scene of desolation after the Vaiont dam disaster.

seemed. It was both foreseeable and, to an extent, foreseen. A report listing shifts in the mountainside and asking for instructions turned up in Rome three days after the slide. The day before, there had been some slight shifts and additional security measures were introduced in the works at the dam. But no one had thought to warn the villagers.

A technical inquiry blamed the accident on the public authorities in the area and on the electricity company responsible for building and operating the dam. It was alleged that the Vaiont dam had been sited in a geologically unsuitable area and that the building work had weakened the mountainside above it.

The disaster caused a delayed death: the director of works at the dam was found dead in a gas-filled room the day before he was due to stand trial on charges of negligence.

Although the dam remains, the area around it has still not recovered from the deluge. Three years after the disaster, a hundred survivors occupied Longarone's new town hall to protest about the slowness of rebuilding their shattered homes.

The tragedy led to an examination of other Alpine dams and artificial lakes, although that did not prevent the death of eighty-eight people, including fifty-six Italians, on 30 August 1965 when a chunk of the Allalin glacier broke away to bury workers building the Mattmark dam, above the Swiss winter sports resort of Saas Fee.

The avalanche crushed the workers' dormitories and canteen, sweeping trucks and bulldozers to destruction. It was not the first time that part of the Allalin glacier had broken away. There was a similar avalanche in 1949, although there seems to have been no local memory of it. In a trial seven years after the disaster, seventeen Swiss engineers and officials were acquitted of charges of homicide by gross negligence.

The Lorado dam: defining a hazard

After the disaster at Aberfan, Wales, in 1966, authorities in many countries checked on the safety of slag heaps that surrounded their mining areas. Nowhere was such a precaution more necessary than in the Appalachians, that area of the United States full of small mine-workings.

The problem there was not so much slag heaps themselves as waste matter that had been piled to form crude dams that held in water used for coal cleaning plants. One of the lessons of Aberfan had been the danger of instability that could result from a combination of coal waste and water. Surveyors, acting under instructions from the Federal Government, discovered in the

An aerial view of the wreckage left after the breaking of the Lorado dam.

Appalachians more than seventy such poorly-built dams. All were dangerous, although that danger was difficult to define in legal terms.

Four years after Aberfan, in 1970, a Federal Act laid down that any impoundment of water at a mine which was deemed a hazard had to be inspected at least once a week by officials of the company responsible for it. The difficulty in enforcing this regulation was that some dams did not reveal that they constituted a hazard until they collapsed.

And collapse they did. According to the U.S. Geological Survey, the lack of regulations made such failures common throughout the Appalachian coal fields. In the six years after Aberfan, there were three dam failures in the Logan and Mingo County areas of West Virginia.

The fourth came on 28 February 1972, killing more than 110 people, injuring 1119, and making more than 6000 homeless. In the flood that followed, the mining camp of Lorado, where 700 lived, was washed away and fifteen other small communities damaged.

The Lorado dam was a crude affair, built of waste material and slate across the mouth of a hollow in the mid-1950s. Behind it, a lake of thick black water extended for 1000 feet across and two miles in length. At the foot of the dam, the water, used in the coal cleaning plant, reached a depth of fifty feet.

The dam broke after a heavy snowfall of more than twenty inches followed by three days of torrential rain. Under this increased pressure, its weak wall gave way, sending a wave of water, thirty feet high, thick with mud and rocks sweeping through Lorado and the other communities of Buffalo Creek Hollow.

The flood of slime travelled eighteen miles in just over an hour, finally emptying into the Guyandotte River. At its height, it was so powerful that some of the dead were found twenty-four miles away from where they had been killed. Many roads disappeared and some 4750 houses were washed away or damaged.

Farnborough 1952: the price of progress

In an age of space travel, it is easy to forget that, not so long ago, there were other aerial obsessions. In the 1950s, the talk was not of reaching other planets but of flying faster than the speed of sound. The 'sound barrier' was something that caught the public's fancy, arousing the curiosity of those who were little interested in flight, just as attempts to run a mile in under four minutes became of more than athletic interest.

There was even a popular novel and film, *The Sound Barrier*, on the theme. But crowds turning up to the Farnborough Air Show in Britain in 1952 were disappointed to learn that no one was to break the barrier for their entertainment.

Just before the Show opened, the organizers banned such flights because of the noise, immense bangs, caused when planes flew at supersonic speeds. This ban was lifted after two days when residents in the area gave assurances that they did not object to the noise.

Whether it was intentional or not, the organizers had made a clever public relations manoeuvre. They had demonstrated that they were not only concerned over causing

Test pilot John Derry and the plane in which he died.

inconvenience to local residents, but also that they were willing to accede to public opinion on the matter.

At first, the pilots had a little trouble. Both John Derry, Britain's first flier to break the barrier, and Squadron Leader Neville Duke, a pilot who had become a celebrity, failed to produce the thunderclaps that usually accompanied supersonic flights.

On 4 September the fourth anniversary of the day on which Derry had first flown faster than sound, he tried again. Watched by a crowd of 120,000, he, together with his observer Tony Richards, took off in a De Havilland 110. Derry dived from 40,000 feet, producing three sonic bangs and then returned to make the usual high speed low-level pass along the runway, about 100 feet

97

John Derry's plane as it hit the ground and began to disintegrate. The body of the pilot can be seen on the far left. The picture was taken by an amateur photographer at Farnborough.

in front of the crowd.

Halfway along, his aeroplane disintegrated. The two engines broke free and continued on their flight path, crashing one and a half miles further on. One hit a hangar. The other sailed in a flaming arc towards Observation Hill, where the spectators were at their densest, packed so tight that those who saw the approaching danger were unable to turn and run. The engine sliced into the crowd, killing twenty-eight. Both Derry and Richards died as their 'plane broke up.

At the inquest into the deaths, the coroner commented: 'Were it not for men prepared to take these risks, progress would not go on.'

4 A captive audience: sporting and entertainment disasters

The blazing wreckage of Pierre Levegh's Mercedes.

Le Mans 1955: death at 155 m.p.h.

Rivalry between three leading motor-car manufacturers, Ferrari, Jaguar, and Mercedes, was at its most intense during the annual twenty-four-hour race at Le Mans in 1955. With many of the finest-ever drivers taking part, commentators anticipated what one described as 'a fantastic speed battle'.

As early as the second lap, records began to go. Juan Fangio, the world champion, broke the lap record in the sixth, ninth, and twenty-second laps, and the Mercedes which he and Stirling Moss were driving was soon well in the lead. But another British driver, Mike Hawthorn, in a Jaguar, went even faster in the twenty-eighth lap, reaching a speed fast enough to travel the eight and a half mile circuit in 4.66 seconds.

On the thirty-sixth lap, Hawthorn was just ahead of a small bunch of cars. Directly behind him was a British driver, Lance

Macklin, driving an Austin Healey at a speed of 127 m.p.h. Then came a Frenchman, Pierre Levegh, a fifty-year-old garage proprietor, driving a silver Mercedes. Following him was Fangio.

Hawthorn slowed to make a pit stop. Levegh, up to 155 m.p.h., raised his arm above his head to indicate that he was going to overtake Macklin. Fangio, also travelling at 155 m.p.h., immediately took his foot off the accelerator, an action that saved his life. For the front of Levegh's car hit the sloping rear of Macklin's and took off, shooting fifteen feet in the air before it hit the protective banking at the edge of the track, where a large crowd stood watching.

The car exploded—'like a magnesium bomb', said an eyewitness. Its rear axle flew into the crowd, decapitating spectators. Others were crushed under the engine and sprayed with burning petrol. Levegh was killed. So were eighty-two of the spectators, and another hundred were seriously injured.

Macklin escaped with a few cuts. Fangio somehow managed to miss Macklin and scrape by Hawthorn, although his car took the green paint off the Jaguar's side.

Charles Faroux, the clerk of the course, decided that the race should continue so that rescue operations would not be hindered by the departure of 250,000 spectators. 'The rough law of sport—and this is a sport like trial by battle—necessitates its continuance', he said later. In a meditation on the catastrophe that he wrote, he added: 'Whatever may be the cost, we must always go further. It is neither possible nor conceivable to set limits to research.'

More than seven hours after the accident, the two remaining Mercedes were withdrawn from the race as a mark of respect to the dead. Hawthorn and his co-driver, Ivor Bueb, went on to win a somewhat hollow victory.

After an exhaustive inquiry, a magistrate decided that no driver was to blame. The decision echoed a remark—'It was fate'—made by Fangio after the race. But, six years later, when, following his retirement, he wrote his autobiography, Fangio changed his mind.

Then, he blamed Hawthorn for unexpectedly braking for his pit stop, causing Macklin to brake and skid and Levegh to crash into him. Hawthorn, claimed Fangio, so misjudged his stop that he ended up eighty yards beyond the pits. It was an accusation that Hawthorn could not answer. He had died in 1959 after crashing his Jaguar on an open road.

Motor-racing was halted throughout Europe for more than four months after Le Mans. In the long term, the disaster led to greater safety for spectators. Now, although motor racing remains the most dangerous of sports, when drivers crash, they usually kill only themselves.

The Lima riot: football as the last refuge of patriotism

Football, especially as played in South America, is less a sport than a means of promoting and expressing national consciousness, a popular culture strong enough to engage the chauvinistic passions of a people.

When an outburst of nationalistic feeling combines with the unthinking behaviour of any crowd, trouble follows. A mob acts

Police throw tear gas bombs at the crowd as the Lima riot begins.

according to the lowest common denominator. A crowd panics easily. At Roosevelt Racecourse in Westbury, New York, in 1971, thirty-seven people were injured in a stampede that started after a soft-drink machine made gurgling noises.

On 26 May 1966 Peru's national football team were playing at home against Argentina at the National Stadium in Lima in a preliminary match for the Olympic Games in Tokyo. Argentina were leading 1–0 when, two minutes before the end, a Peruvian winger broke through and scored. The Uruguayian referee disallowed the goal because of rough play.

The crowd of more than 45,000 shouted and screamed their disapproval. Some spectators leapt over the barriers to attack the referee and were arrested. As the booing reached a crescendo, the referee suspended the game.

Frustrated and enraged, the crowd crashed through the barriers and swarmed on to the pitch. Had this mob caught up with the players and the referee, it is unlikely that they would have escaped alive. But they ran to lock themselves behind the thick steel door of a locker room and police later smuggled them out of the stadium.

The few police on duty—there were no more than forty—were as panicky as the crowd. Mounted police used tear-gas as others loosed dogs on to the mob, drew their revolvers and fired into the air. At least four people died in the fusillade.

Confused and fearful, under attack and charged by the mounted police, many people tried to flee the stadium by the few exit doors that were not still locked. They fought among themselves and the weaker were trampled underfoot and asphyxiated. The crowd smashed every window in the stadium,

The end of the riot. Relatives move among the bodies trying to identify the dead.

surging into the streets and sacking stores, burning buildings, and overturning cars.

Thieves made the most of the opportunity to steal wallets, jewelry, and other valuables from the dying and the injured scattered over the pitch. By the time the carnage ended, there were 300 dead and 500 injured.

A nurse runs into Ibrox Park to help the injured.

Bolton and Ibrox: the little additional influences

The inquiry into the panic at the football ground of the English team Bolton Wanderers, a panic which killed thirty-three people, reported:

How simple and how easy it is for a dangerous situation to arise in a crowded enclosure. It happens again and again without fatal or even injurious con-

Bodies of the victims lie covered on the ground at Burnham Park after the Bolton disaster.

sequences. But its danger is that it requires so little additional influences—an involuntary sway, an exciting moment, a comparatively small addition to the crowd, the failure of one part of one barrier—to translate the danger into terms of death and injuries. The pastime of football watching is on the increase and the chances of danger among the crowds are rising.

That statement was made in 1945. It was as true on 2 January 1971 in the last seconds of the traditional New Year's game between Glasgow Rangers and Celtic at Ibrox Park, Glasgow, a game so partisan in its violence that the supporters of the two teams were segregated. Four years earlier the date of the match had been shifted from New Year's Day in an attempt to curb the often drunken exuberance of the crowd.

As the game drew to an end, Celtic were winning 1–0 and disappointed Rangers' supporters had begun to leave. Almost on the final whistle, Rangers equalized. Alerted by the cheers, fans turned back to discover what had happened. As they did so, they ran into a mass of people coming down the terraces.

One boy threw his scarf into the air in joy; another, his anorak. When they bent down to pick them up they were pushed from behind and fell forward on the stairway that led to Terrace no. 13. This sudden move unbalanced everyone, and the railings gave way under the unexpected pressure.

One spectator remembers being pulled out of his shoes in the crush. Another blacked out and recovered to find his brother standing beside him, dead. In the mêlée, sixty-six people died and 170 were injured. An exciting moment, an involuntary sway, had been translated into death.

At Ibrox, the attendance was strictly limited to 80,000. At Bolton Wanderers, on 9 March 1945 there was no such limit. Officials had expected a crowd of around 50,000, but 85,000 turned up. At the most popular part of the ground, the Railway Enclosure, the pressure was so great that some spectators on the crest found themselves squeezed down to the bottom in a few minutes, despite their resistance.

The order to close the turnstiles came too late to stop overcrowding. A policeman realized the dangers and tried to open some of the exit gates to relieve the pressure, but he could find no one with the necessary keys.

In the heaving mass of people, a child became hysterical. His father, trying to take him out of the ground, found that the nearest exit was padlocked. He picked the lock and hustled his son away. Outside, those who had been locked out rushed through the open door. Some 3000 added to the crush in the Railway Enclosure.

At this moment, the teams of Bolton and Stoke City ran on to the pitch, and the game began. As the mass of people pushed and shoved for a vantage point, two barriers gave way near the corner flag. The crowd fell forward; yet there were so many that they made no gap. There was merely a sinking movement, the ripple of a wave that ran from the back to the front. People were heaped four deep on top of one another and trampled underfoot.

Apart from the thirty-three dead, there were 500 injured. The game, which had been stopped after twelve minutes of play, was re-started and the teams played through without the usual interval.

One of the injured was so affected that, seven months later, he attempted to commit suicide because he felt worthless. He lost his memory and it was four and a half years before he was fully recovered. Of the match, he could remember nothing, but spoke of being badly injured in a cyclone and trampled by a herd of elephants.

The Knickerbocker Cinema cave-in: snow on snow

The worst snow storm for years hit Washington D.C. on 28 January 1922, falling heavily, continually throughout the day. By the evening, the snow lay twenty-eight inches deep.

At the Knickerbocker, one of the city's

newest and largest cinemas, the management wondered about the weight of the snow on the roof before deciding that it was safe enough.

After a fall of plaster, the roof gave way at 9 p.m., falling on 500 people. The balcony, too, collapsed, throwing 100 down into the stalls and causing one of the building's exterior walls to cave in.

The collapse killed 120 of the audience, including eleven couples and the conductor of the cinema's orchestra. There were a few lucky escapes: two children were found asleep under a pile of dead bodies.

The disaster, decided a coroner's jury, was due to the cinema's faulty design and construction and to the lack of adequate supervision and inspection.

Rescuers hunt for survivors amidst the wreckage of the Knickerbocker Cinema.

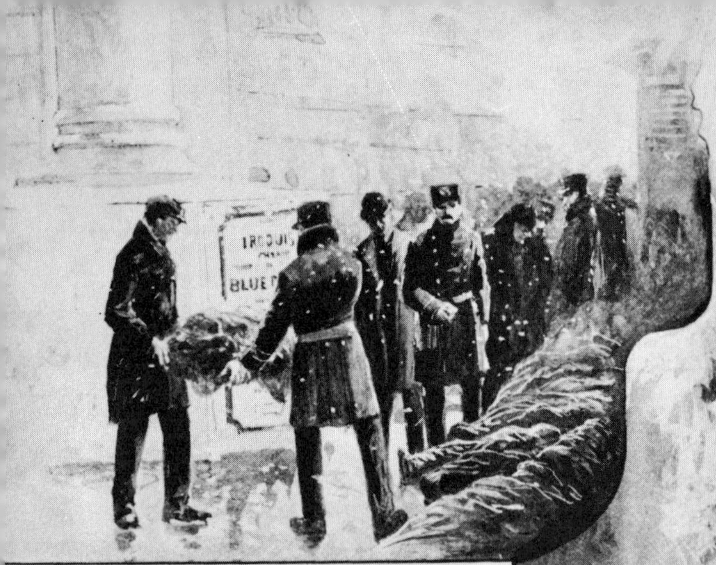

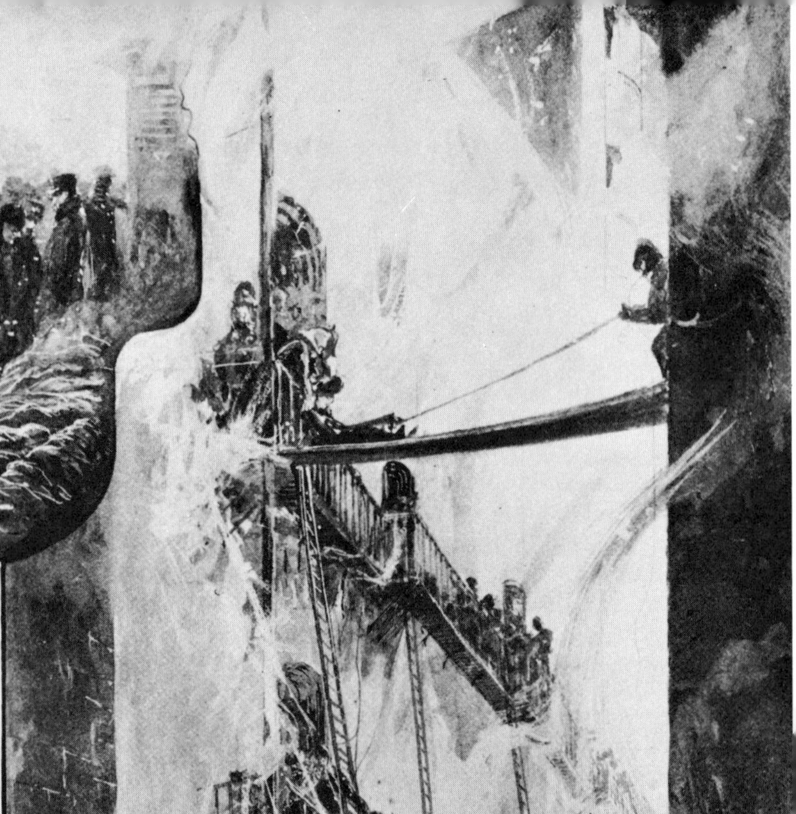

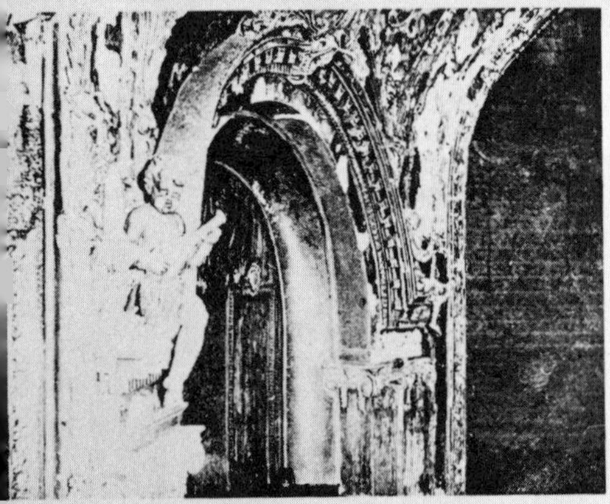

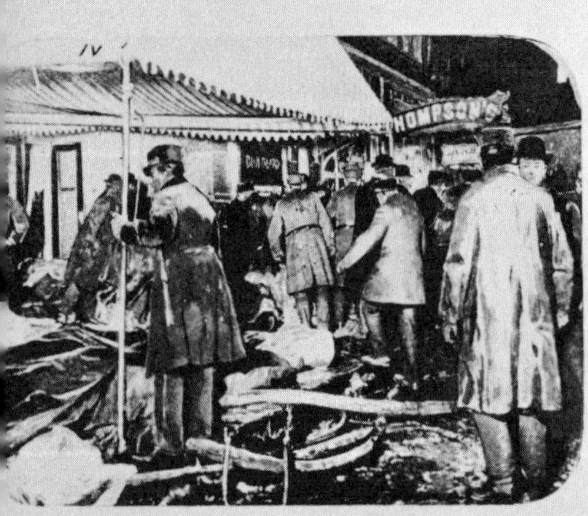
IV

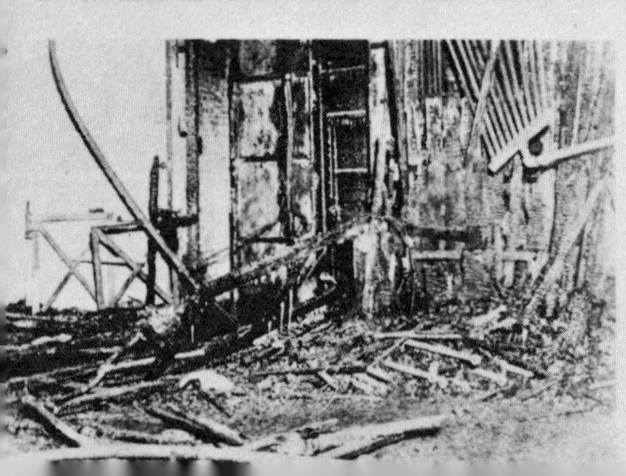

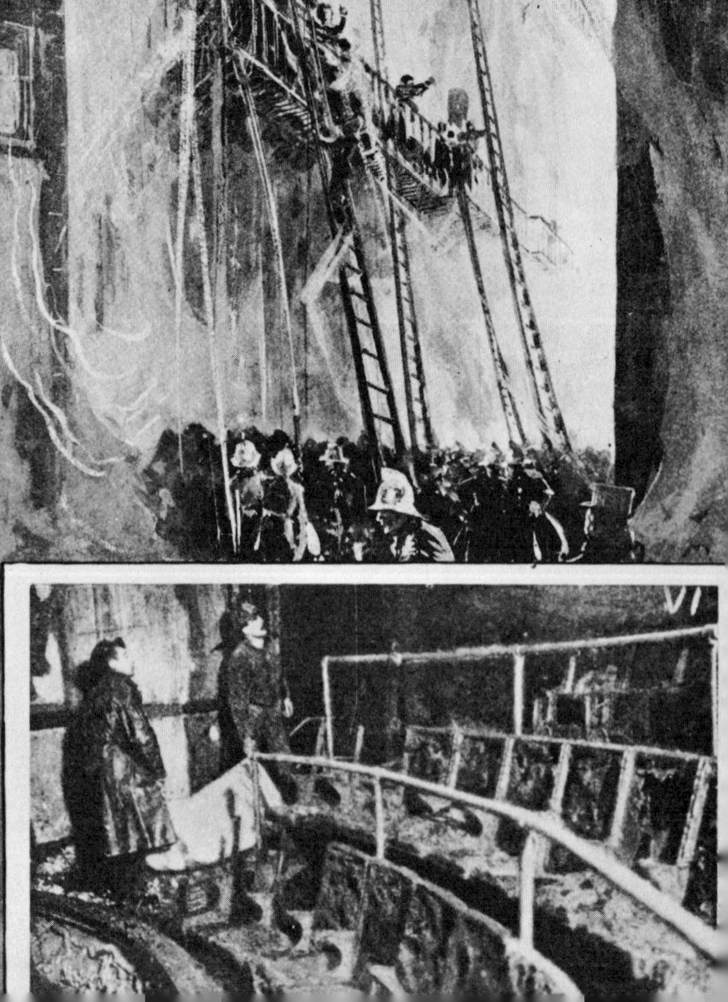
VI

The Iroquois Theatre fire: entrances and exits

The day the Iroquois Theatre in Chicago burned down—it was 30 December 1903—came five weeks after the building had been opened to the public. It should not have opened at all, for it was not ready on time, and work continued between performances. But the owners, anxious to begin to recoup their investment, were also certain of one point: the theatre was fireproof. They had spent a great deal of money to ensure that, installing an asbestos safety curtain, something few theatres possessed.

Someone, though, had also gone to the trouble of spreading a little money among the city officials responsible for enforcing fire regulations. That was normal practice in Chicago. After the disastrous blaze at the Iroquois, it was discovered that only one theatre in the locality conformed to the city ordinances.

There was a packed house of 1300 when the fire broke out, on a small scale at first. It started when an operator changed one of the incandescent lights from white to blue, to simulate moonlight for a dance sequence. The electric arc between the light's carbons spluttered, and a spark set fire to the frayed edge of a curtain.

Some stagehands rushed on with fire extinguishers. Unfortunately, the management had neglected to give their staff any instructions on how they were to act in case of fire. They were unable to control the blaze, and the flames caught the scenery, which was quickly alight, and ran along 75,000 feet of oiled rope which was used to haul up and down the backdrops.

The fire was fierce, but, at that point, did not much worry the audience. They had not panicked and were keeping their seats, as they had been asked to by one of the performers. Trouble began with the lowering of the asbestos safety curtain to cut off the stage from the auditorium.

The curtain was cumbersome, for it had to be hauled down by means of a rope. And it stuck. Later, the management claimed that it had bellied because of the draught caused by the fire. The real reason was carelessness. One side had become entangled in a light at the top of the proscenium arch. There were two powerful spotlights, one each side of the arch, that swung out to illumine the stage. When they were in position they blocked the descent of the safety curtain.

So the curtain stuck with one end five feet from the stage and the other still some twenty-five feet in the air. This coupled with the draught from the many doorways into the theatre—there were forty entrances in all—turned the stage into an excellent chimney.

Just before the safety curtain came down, many of the audience in the balconies had pressed forward in order to get a better view of the fire. When the curtain jammed, the draught caused huge flames to lick out beneath it, reaching the balcony and setting people and draperies alight. The panic began.

Scenes from the fire at the Iroquois theatre. *From top:* bringing out the dead; firemen working on the rescue-bridge at the rear of the theatre; ruined decorations in the auditorium; the scene in front of the theatre an hour after the fire; the ruins of the stage; rescuers at work in the gallery.

The balcony was so steep that as people ran to escape, pushing and fighting, many were knocked backwards into the flames. A great many victims were women and children who were trampled to death. Others died so quickly, of asphyxiation, that they were found still sitting in their seats.

Around the exit from the balcony, firemen found bodies piled for thirteen feet. In the centre, the bodies reached to two feet below the ceiling of the passageway. They were so tightly jammed between the walls and the sides of the narrow exit that it was impossible to disentangle a single body.

Some unfortunates ran out of a fire escape only to discover that it led nowhere but to an iron balcony. The ladder leading to the ground, some fifty feet beneath, had not been built. Those in front were pushed off, down to the pavement below, by people pressing from behind, who, in turn, found themselves fighting a mob to stay alive. At least twenty-five people died in this manner.

Eleven other emergency exits were finished, but their doors were bolted. The fire killed 587 people. Most of the performers escaped, due to the coolheadedness of the show's star, Eddie Foy, and to a liftboy, who took his elevator up to a gallery to rescue some trapped chorus girls.

There seems to have been a little local indifference to the fire. Chicago's livery-stable drivers, then engaged in a protracted strike, refused to take out carriages in order to help remove the dead and injured from the theatre. And at least a dozen people were arrested after they were caught robbing the corpses.

But its effect was felt all over the world, as the public insisted on more stringent fire regulations. It led to the closing of the Royal Opera House, Berlin, while that theatre was made safer for audiences.

The Cocoanut Grove fire: a misplaced match

The Cocoanut Grove, one of Boston's most popular night clubs, tried to live up to its name. The interior décor featured plenty of palm trees, not, of course, real but artificial and, as it happened, highly inflammable.

On 28 November 1942, the club was packed by a thousand people. At 10.15 p.m., one of the workers, a fifteen-year-old boy, was trying to replace a light bulb that some merrymaker had removed, presumably as a joke. He lit a match so that he could see what he was doing, and threw it aside. It fell on to an artificial palm, just inside the entrance, which flared immediately.

The decorations burned quickly so that the fire spread to block the way out. People rushed to one of the emergency exits and found that it was bolted. The windows at the back of the building had been boarded up. Soon, the dead and the dying blocked those doors and windows that were barred.

Many managed to climb on to the roof and jump to safety, for it was a low building. The club's manager, with ten others, sheltered in the basement icebox. But 492 died and another 170 were badly injured.

The following day, police had to block roads leading in to Boston in order to keep out hoards of sightseers.

The fire at St Laurent du Pont: death in quick time

Le Cinq-Sept dance hall at St Laurent du Pont, a small French town near Grenoble, seemed to have been designed as a fire-trap *par excellence*.

The hall was little more than a barn, built mainly of wood. It had no windows. The dancing area was surrounded by grottoes made of plastic backed with cardboard. The ceiling was covered by plastic tiles, the chairs were of cardboard with cushions made from synthetic material.

There was no telephone. There was no water supply. Three of the four emergency exits were not only padlocked, but also had planks nailed across them to discourage gate-crashers. The other exit was virtually inaccessible. There was only one way out or in, through an entrance fitted with metal barriers and a turnstile.

A young, mainly teenage audience came to the dances. On 1 November 1970 some 300 turned up. By 1.45 a.m. there were still nearly 150 left. Someone threw away a lighted match. It fell on a cushion which

The burned-out interior of the dance hall at St Laurent du Pont.

caught fire. Almost immediately, the chair blazed and, in a moment, the polystyrene and polyurethane decorations flamed from one end of the hall to the other, raining burning plastic down upon the dancers.

Firemen reached the hall after ten minutes. It was so quiet that at first they believed that everyone had escaped. But, behind the main entrance, they found bodies lying six feet deep. Some couples had been overwhelmed so quickly that they had died in each other's arms on the dance floor.

Six of those inside the hall escaped through the one emergency door that was open, but which lay concealed behind the bar.

St Laurent du Pont is a small town, with a population of under 4000. On an average day 5000 people drive through it in their cars. On 2 November the numbers swelled to 60,000 cars filled with curious people.

Investigations revealed that the hall should never have been opened to the public. The owners had not sought the necessary official permission to operate it for dancing. Nor had it ever been inspected by the fire department.

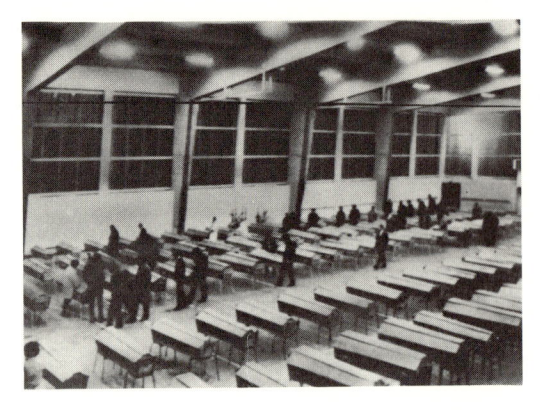

Rows of coffins of the young victims of the fire lie in a specially-prepared chapel in the local school gymnasium.

The Indiana State Fair explosion: death on ice

The audience were late in arriving at the 'Holiday on Ice' show at the Indiana State Fair Coliseum on Thursday, 31 October 1963. It was Hallowe'en, and the excited and chattering children, coming to the show after parties, delayed the start by fifteen minutes. Even then, the stadium, which held 8000, was little more than half full.

Usually the show ended just before 11 p.m. This night, at 11.06 p.m., when the rink would have been emptying of its audience, everyone was still in their seats, enjoying the climax of the entertainment. Suddenly, there was a gigantic explosion from the refreshment buffet, as propane gas was ignited by a lighted cigarette end.

The force of the explosion hurled bodies seventy feet in the air to crash against the ceiling, and broke concrete slabs two feet thick, sending them smashing across the rink. The ice melted and ran red with blood, as sixty died and another 300 were injured.

To still the panic, while people were recovering from the shock and bodies were being laid out on the ice for identification, the show's band played a rousing version of the dixieland tune, *South Rampart Street Parade*.

5 The way the world ends: explosion and fire

Halifax, Ardey, and Cali: bangs and whimpers

In the harbour of Halifax, Novia Scotia, a munitions ship and a steamer collided, through a misunderstanding of signals. The captain of the munitions ship managed just before the collision to manoeuvre his vessel so that the hold containing explosives was not hit.

But the impact upset twenty barrels of benzol which poured on to some acid in a hold beneath and ignited it. Before they fled, the crew desperately tried to sink the ship. Their attempt was unsuccessful. At 9 a.m. on 7 December 1917 the ship blew up.

The blast levelled most of the north end of the city, and was seen and heard by ships at sea more than fifty miles away. Two square

Below and opposite
Views of the devastation following the two explosions at the Ardey, Westphalia, Roburite factory.

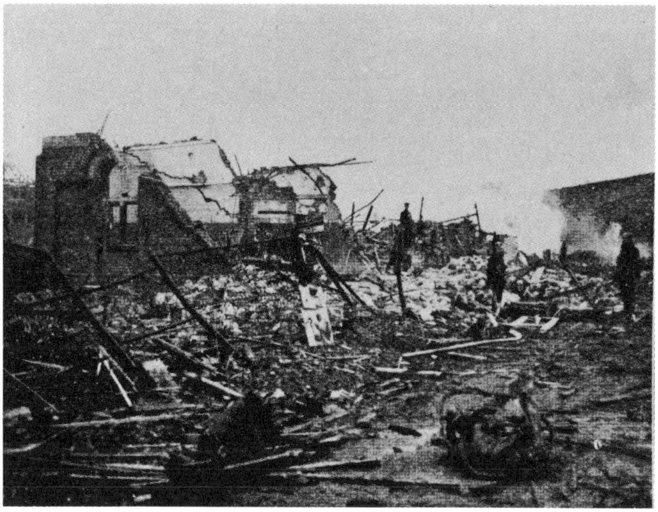

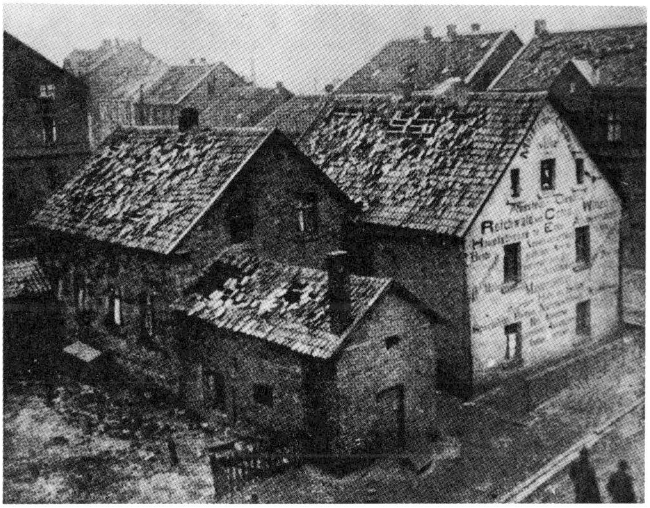

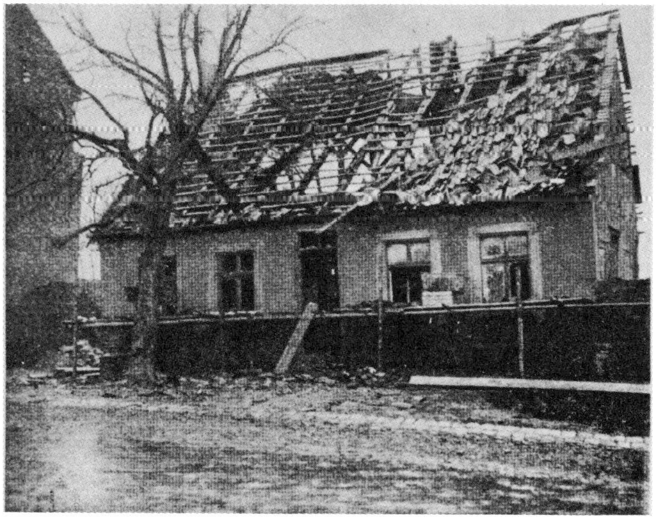

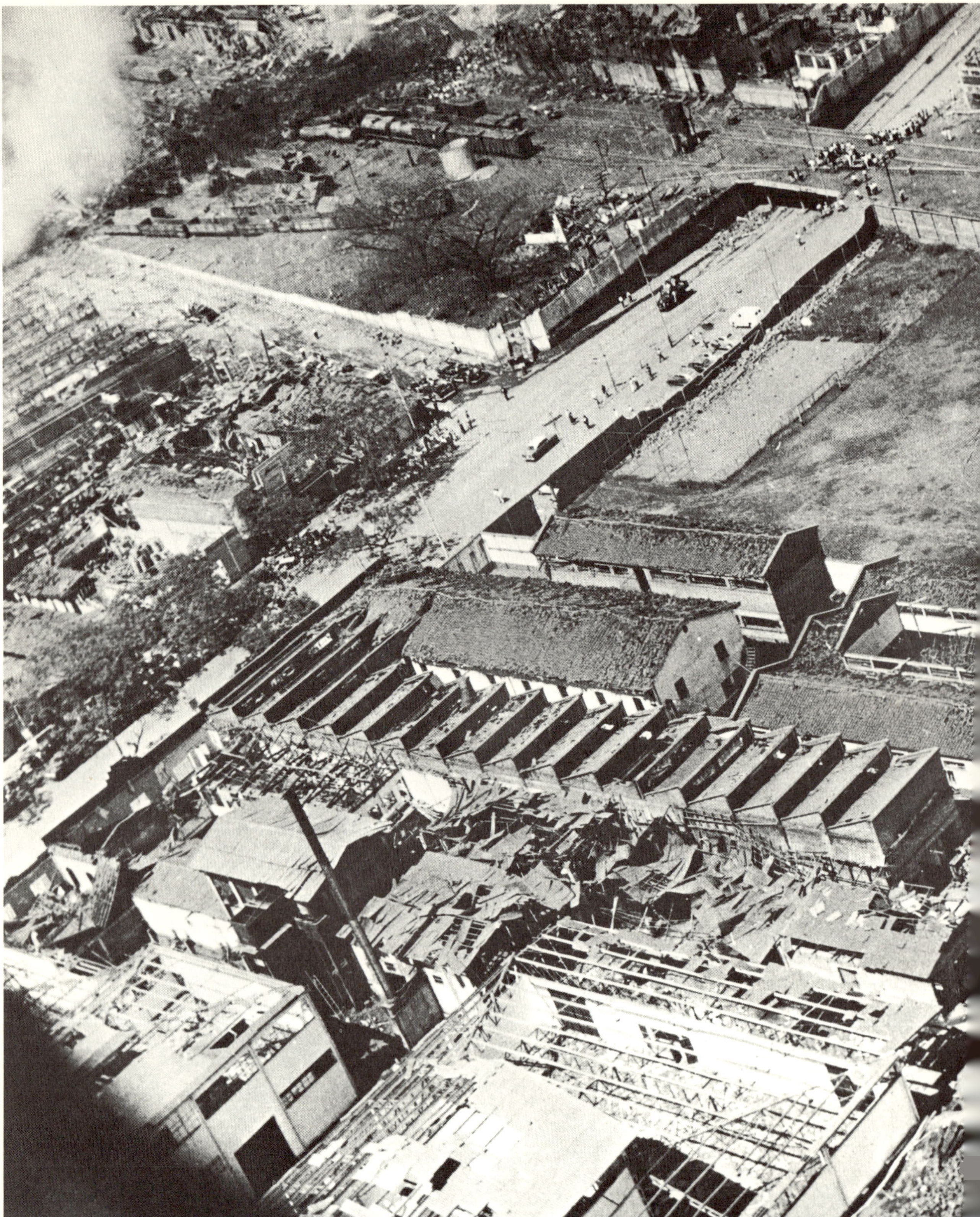

miles of the city burned to the ground, destroying 3000 homes and causing $30,000,000 (£11,500,000) damage.

Rescuers were hindered by the severe snow storm that soon followed, with three feet of snow falling on the wrecked city. In one school not far from the harbour, they found the bodies of 200 children.

No one knows how many died, although it is probable that the coroner overestimated when he ordered 4000 coffins. At least 1200 died, possibly as many as 3000, and 8000 were injured, many seriously. More than 300 people were blinded by flying glass.

But the lesson of Halifax was obvious: explosives should be kept away from densely populated areas. That lesson could have been learned eleven years earlier, when an explosion wrecked the Ardey Roburite works in Westphalia, on 28 November 1906.

That blast brought many running to the wrecked works, some to offer help, others to gape. After a large crowd had gathered, there was a second, more devastating explosion.

The two small towns nearby, Witten and Annen, were largely destroyed by the explosion after fires broke out. Twenty-eight people died, and 150 were injured.

The lesson had still not been learned by 7 August 1956 when eight trucks containing dynamite exploded at Cali, Colombia, killing 1100 people as they lay sleeping, and injuring another 2000. Those that died were 'soldiers and humble people', said the President of Colombia as he ordered three days of national mourning.

An aerial view of the huge explosion at Cali, Colombia, showing the ruined army barracks where 500 sleeping soldiers died.

The Pittsburg explosion: the biggest gasometer in the world

There are plenty of jokes about the dangers of looking for a gas leak with a naked flame. The workmen repairing the biggest gasometer in the world, at Pittsburg, Pennsylvania, went one better. They used a blow lamp.

Not long after they started work, at 10 a.m. on 14 November 1927, the tank, which contained five million cubic feet of natural gas, blew up, killing twenty-eight, most of them from a nearby factory, and injuring 500.

An eyewitness said that the tank rose in the air like a balloon before exploding, as if it were a firework bomb. Chunks of metal, some of them weighing more than 100 lb. were found a mile away.

People nearby who rushed into the streets from their shaking houses were driven back by what seemed like a wall of searing flame. A square mile of Pittsburg's industrial centre was devastated and 4000 people were made homeless. On a roof not far away, used for weather forecasting, the blast so affected the air pressure that the barometer went up $\frac{5}{16}$ in.

The flattened industrial centre of Pittsburg following the explosion of the largest gasometer in the world, reduced to a smoking ruin, *left*. *Right* an aerial view of the gas-tank and the wreckage it caused.

The Silvertown explosion: a stern necessity

The Silvertown explosion on 19 January 1917, which wrecked a chemical factory, a flour mill, and three streets of cramped, terraced houses in London's East End, was powerful enough for its shock to be registered 122 miles away. In Slough, only twenty-five miles away, people who heard the rumble and saw a red glow in the sky thought that a zeppelin had crashed.

The disaster began with a fire starting in a factory manufacturing high explosives for use in the war against Germany. The cause was never established, although it is known that the fire broke out in the building's small top floor where only two people worked. Both were among the seventy-three who died. It could be that one of them broke the works' strict 'no smoking' rule—anyone caught smoking was instantly sacked—although an inquiry decided that the fire began accidentally, possibly through spontaneous combustion.

A fire station stood next door to the factory. At a little before 7 p.m. the alarm sounded and, within a few minutes, firemen were trying to put out the blaze. Seven minutes after the alarm came the explosion, wrecking the fire engine and killing two firemen. Sixty-nine people died instantly, ninety-four were seriously injured, another 328 needed hospital treatment, and some 600 attended to their own cuts and bruises.

Where the factory had stood, there was a large smoking crater. The blast also demolished every house within a 400 yard radius. The destruction was on a horrific scale. A mother was nursing her eighteen-month-old baby in her kitchen when the house collapsed upon her, killing the child and her husband. Another man who died had the skin practically stripped from his body.

One of the workers from the flour mill, injured by flying glass, ran to the ruins of his home to try to save his mother. He found her lying under a pile of bricks. She was blinded and had lost a leg. She died in hospital the next day.

The damage done by the explosion was put at £2,250,000 ($5,850,000). More than a thousand people were made homeless and many children orphaned. Some of them were offered places in The Home for Working Boys, which announced that it could place any children aged fourteen or over in immediate jobs.

The explosion was followed by wild rumours that a German worker in the factory had set fire to it, and some claimed that the chief chemist—a man named Angel—was of German descent. These stories of sabotage were met with an official denial. Indeed, Angel heroically went to help the firemen after warning his colleagues of the fire, and he died in the blast.

Although the cause of the accident was deemed to be accidental, there was an equally serious question that needed answering: what was a factory full of high explosives doing in one of London's most densely populated areas, where working-class families lived in overcrowded conditions?

The government's explanation was brief: 'stern necessity', said a spokesman. The factory was the only place in Britain which could provide the necessary knowledge and skill to manufacture high explosives. Speed was essential because of the war, and there was no time to even consider shifting the factory or its personnel. It was an answer that seemed to satisfy people at the time.

The Reichstag fire: a small but terrible conflagration

Marinus van der Lubbe, a Dutchman of limited intelligence and left-wing opinions, nurtured a burning desire to set fire to the Reichstag building in Berlin, home of the German Parliament. It was a predilection he shared with an Austrian of overweening ambition: Adolf Hitler, then Chancellor of Germany, a position he gained in January, 1933.

Hitler was engaged on a campaign to intimidate his enemies so that the Nazis might come to power in a general election which had been fixed for March. He thrived in an atmosphere of plot and intrigue. If the Reichstag were fired, and if the Communists were blamed, then he would be provided with the opportunity to stifle his left-wing opponents for ever.

The exact details of the plans to burn the Reichstag have never come to light, although at the Nuremburg trials after World War II there was plenty of evidence that it was planned by the Nazis. Van der Lubbe's role is as obscure. Beforehand, he boasted of trying to burn down other buildings in Berlin and said that the next time he would set fire to the Reichstag. Perhaps he put the notion into the minds of the Nazi leaders. Certainly, he provided the perfect scapegoat, being both dim-witted and Communist. Perhaps, too, he was encouraged by the Nazis. Whatever the reason, on the night of 27 February 1933 he entered the Reichstag and started a fire there by setting light to his shirt.

His pitiful attempt at arson was hardly necessary. For fires were lit in several parts of the building at the same time, using cloth soaked in petrol and chemicals. Indeed, the Reichstag's main hall was ablaze almost as soon as van der Lubbe entered the building.

During the Nuremburg trials, Goebbels, then shortly to become Hitler's Minister of Propaganda, was credited with planning the fire. He prepared in advance a list of those to be arrested in the furore that would follow. Goering, too, has been held responsible, although he denied it.

Goering was one of the first to arrive at the fire, screaming that it was a Communist plot and that all of the Communist deputies of the Reichstag should be hanged or shot immediately. Soon after, Hitler, who had been dining with Goebbels, arrived with his host. He, too, had no doubt that it was the work of Communists and vowed that nothing would stop him crushing them with an iron fist.

Within a few hours, a state of emergency was declared in order to protect the Reich against the Communist danger. Swiftly, all the Communist deputies of the Reichstag were rounded up and imprisoned.

The next day, Hitler persuaded President Hindenburg to issue a decree stating that 'restrictions on personal liberty, on the right of free expression of opinion, including freedom of the press; on the rights of assembly and association; and violations of the privacy of postal, telegraphic, and telephonic communications; and warrants for house searches, orders for confiscations as well as restrictions on property are also permissible beyond the legal limit otherwise prescribed.'

These severe restrictions on individual liberty remained in force throughout the Third Reich's existence, forming the basis for a police state. With more than 4000 liberal and left-wing leaders being arrested, the general election was held in an atmosphere of hysteria and fear. The Nazis broke up meetings organized by their opponents and harassed them in other ways.

Even so, Hitler failed to gain an over-all majority at the general election, although the

The Reichstag, home of the German Parliament, in flames.

Nazi vote showed a sizeable increase and the Communist vote a decline. But the Reichstag fire had given him the opportunity to crush his opponents and to create a situation that enabled him to seize complete power within a month.

The trial of the alleged arsonists became an irrelevance. Van der Lubbe was accused, together with Ernst Togler, a leading German Communist, and three Bulgarian Communists. The Bulgarians were acquitted, Togler was imprisoned, and van der Lubbe executed.

The actual incendiary seems to have been Karl Ernst, leader of the Berlin S.A., the Brownshirts, and three of his men. They entered and left the Reichstag through a tunnel connecting the building to Goering's official residence. Just over a year later, on 30 June 1934 all four were murdered during Hitler's brutal purge of the Brownshirts.

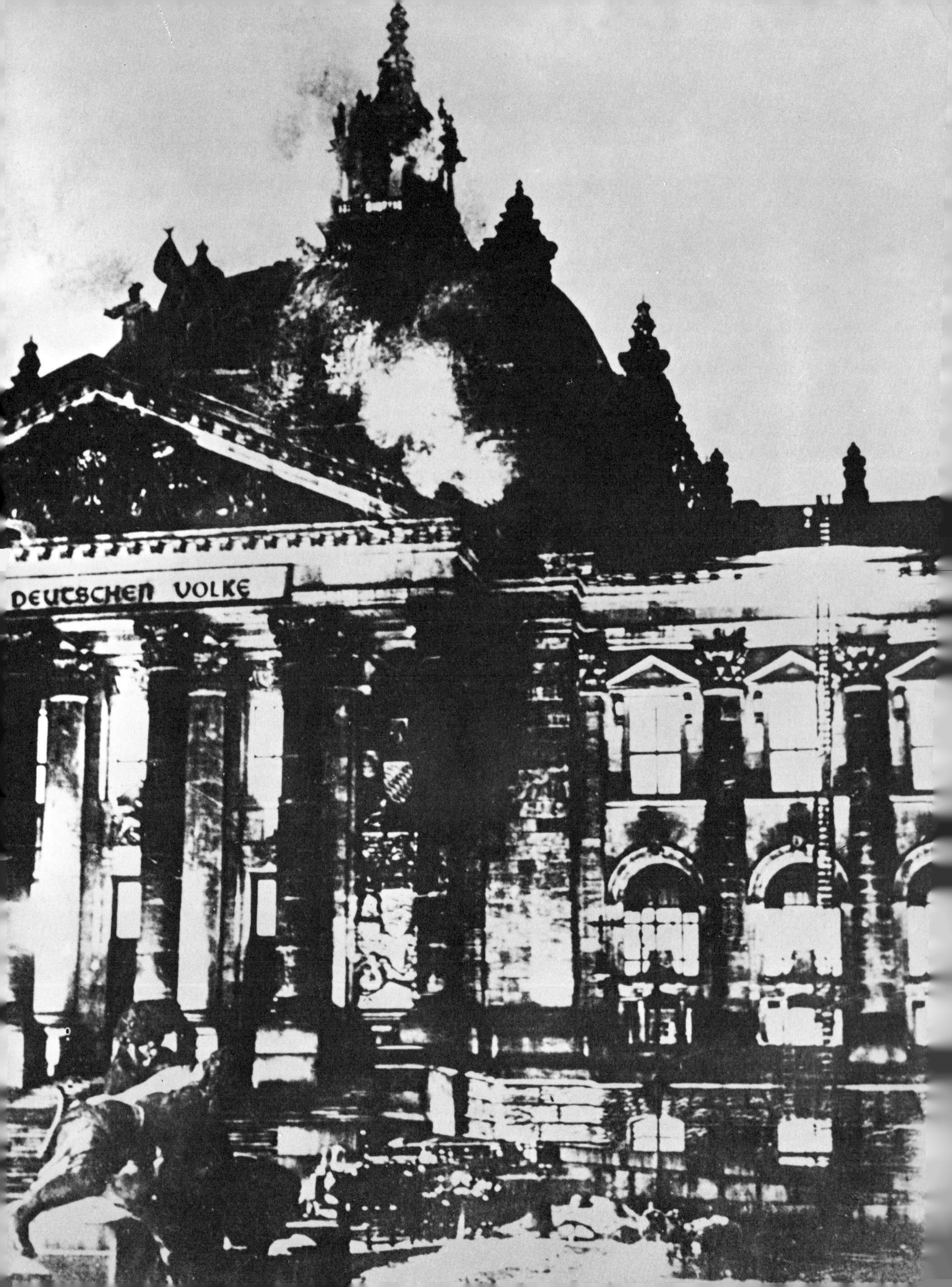
DEUTSCHEN VOLKE

Firemen trying to extinguish the Reichstag blaze.

The Fontanet explosion: a delayed bang

In Cincinatti and Indianapolis people thought that the slight shock they felt at 9.15 a.m. on 15 October 1907 was an earthquake. But sixty-five miles away from the capital, the inhabitants of the small town of Fontanet, Indiana, knew the even grimmer truth.

For it was at that moment that the Dupont Glazing Mill, a mile away from the town, blew up. It was a danger the townspeople lived with. Many were employed at the Dupont Blasting Powder Mills and knew the risks of working with gunpowder.

The first blast killed several workers. As the noise of the explosion still reverberated, men ran for their lives from the nearby mills and the townsfolk fled their homes, seeking the safety of the open streets. As the rush began, two other mills exploded, raining debris down on the fleeing workers, killing some and injuring many more.

The three explosions caused great devastation and fire. Rescuers quickly moved into the wrecked area to aid the wounded and discover the dead. But the worst was still to come.

At 10.45 a.m. the Mills' powder magazine, built in a hollow a quarter of a mile away, suddenly blew up. Some 65,000 kegs of powder exploded, setting fire to a freight train in a nearby siding and shattering the windows in another train some four miles away, injuring several passengers.

The series of explosions wrecked every building within half a mile radius, as well as totally destroying a farmhouse nearly a mile away and two churches. In Fontanet itself, many houses collapsed. In a school a quarter of a mile away, fifty children were injured as the walls caved in. In a two-room schoolhouse two miles away, ninety children were buried as the roof gave way, although none were seriously injured.

In all, 1200 people were made homeless, 600 were injured and thirty-one died. The explosions caused $280,000,000 (£108,000,000) damage to the Mills and another $500,000 (£192,000) worth to the town of Fontanet.

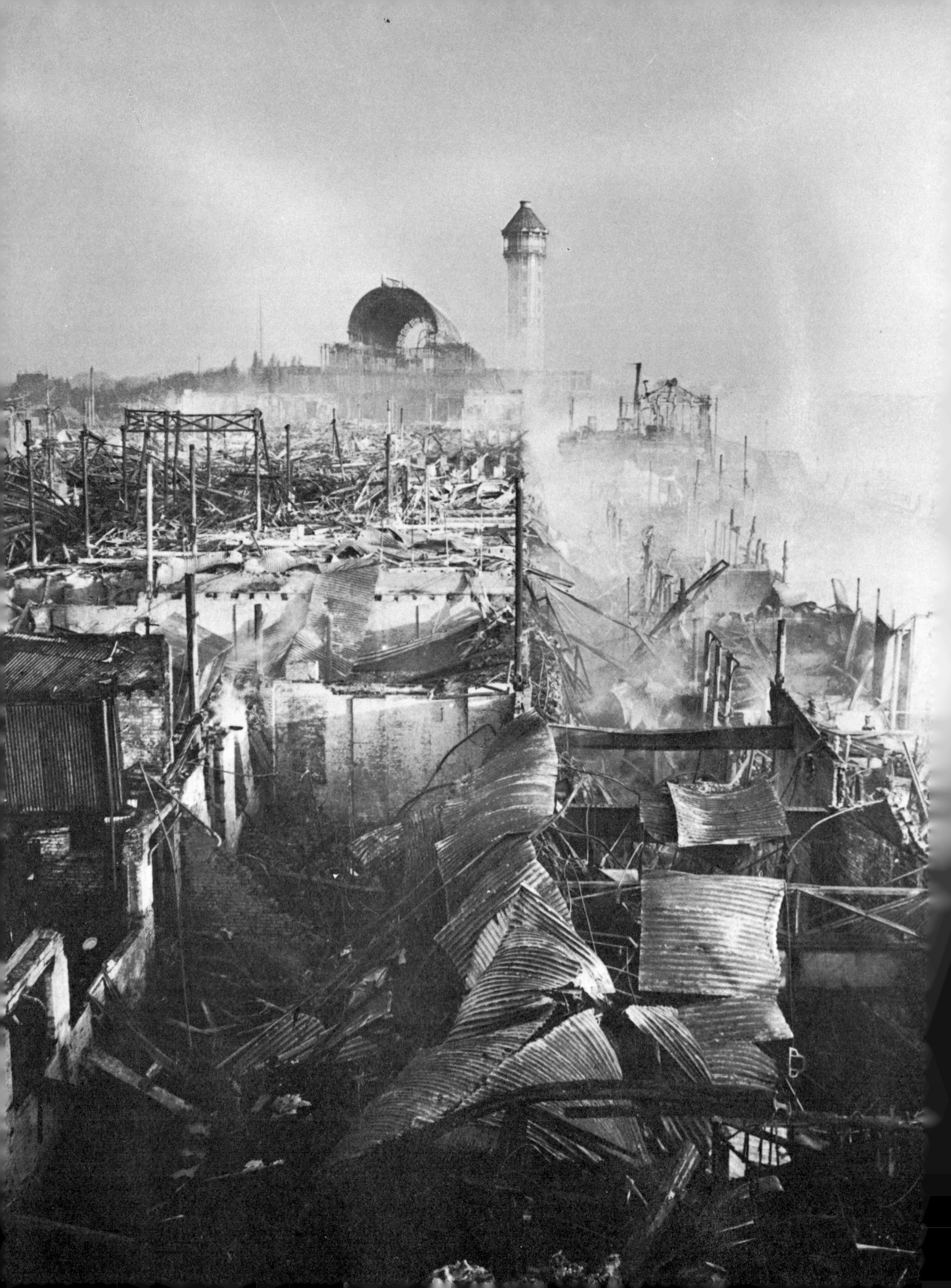

The smoking remains of the Coney Island fire that destroyed thirty acres of New York's favourite pleasure-resort.

Coney Island and Crystal Palace: playgrounds of fire

Some fires, although they involve little loss of life, are still on a disastrous scale. So it was at New York's playground, Coney Island, on 28 July 1907. Two people died. But the flames consumed most of the amusement arcades, four hotels, and other buildings, causing $1,000,000 (£385,000) damage.

So it was at London's playground, the Crystal Palace, that huge glass pleasure-dome that had first stood in Hyde Park for the Great Exhibition of 1851, the glittering centrepiece of the reign of Queen Victoria. After the exhibition, the building was sold for £70,000 ($182,000) and rebuilt, on a larger scale, on Sydenham Hill.

The new palace was 2756 feet long. The central hall was nearly 1600 feet long with two high towers, the only parts of the build-

After the great fire, only the tower of the Crystal Palace still stands.

125

The smoking ruins of what was Brussels' largest department store.

ing that escaped the fire that began at 7.30 p.m. on Monday, 30 November 1936.

The palace was so built that it formed a natural flue for any fire, and, within half an hour, it was ablaze and it went on burning, despite the attentions of 400 firemen and ninety fire-engines, through the night. The flames rose 150 feet in the air and their glow could be seen thirty miles away.

L'Innovation fire: let the buyer beware

Was it sabotage caused by anti-American feeling, or merely an accident that led to the deaths of 322 people and the destruction of Brussels' largest department store, L'Innovation, on 22 May 1967.

The store was featuring an 'American Week', which had been denounced by a Maoist group who distributed pamphlets attacking the United States to shoppers. Someone had 'phoned the police, claiming that a bomb had been planted, although a search had revealed nothing.

No evidence of sabotage was ever discovered in the smoking ruins of the store after the fire, which caused damage totalling £7,000,000 ($18,000,000), had burned itself out. It started when a gas cylinder exploded in a camping equipment exhibition on the third floor. The time was the lunch hour, when more than a thousand customers were in the store. The flames soon trapped those who were on the four floors above. Fourteen shoppers jumped to their deaths from the roof down to the narrow rue Neuve below. Others escaped by clambering on to neighbouring buildings.

Before long the store's glass roof collapsed, turning its central well into a huge chimney. One wall collapsed into the street as the nearby buildings also went up in flames.

One of the firemen described the scene: 'I picked up one poor woman who jumped out of a second floor window and shattered both legs on the pavement underneath. One man was transformed into a living torch before my eyes as he hesitated to leap from a high window ledge.'

The next day, an anonymous caller told the police that a bomb had been planted in another of Brussels' large stores. The shop was evacuated, but the call proved to be a hoax.

The Glasgow fire: caught behind bars

There are many warehouses near the city centre of Glasgow. The one in James Watt Street had been a whisky bond and showed signs of an acute concern for security. At every window, there were thick iron bars.

Another firm had taken over the building

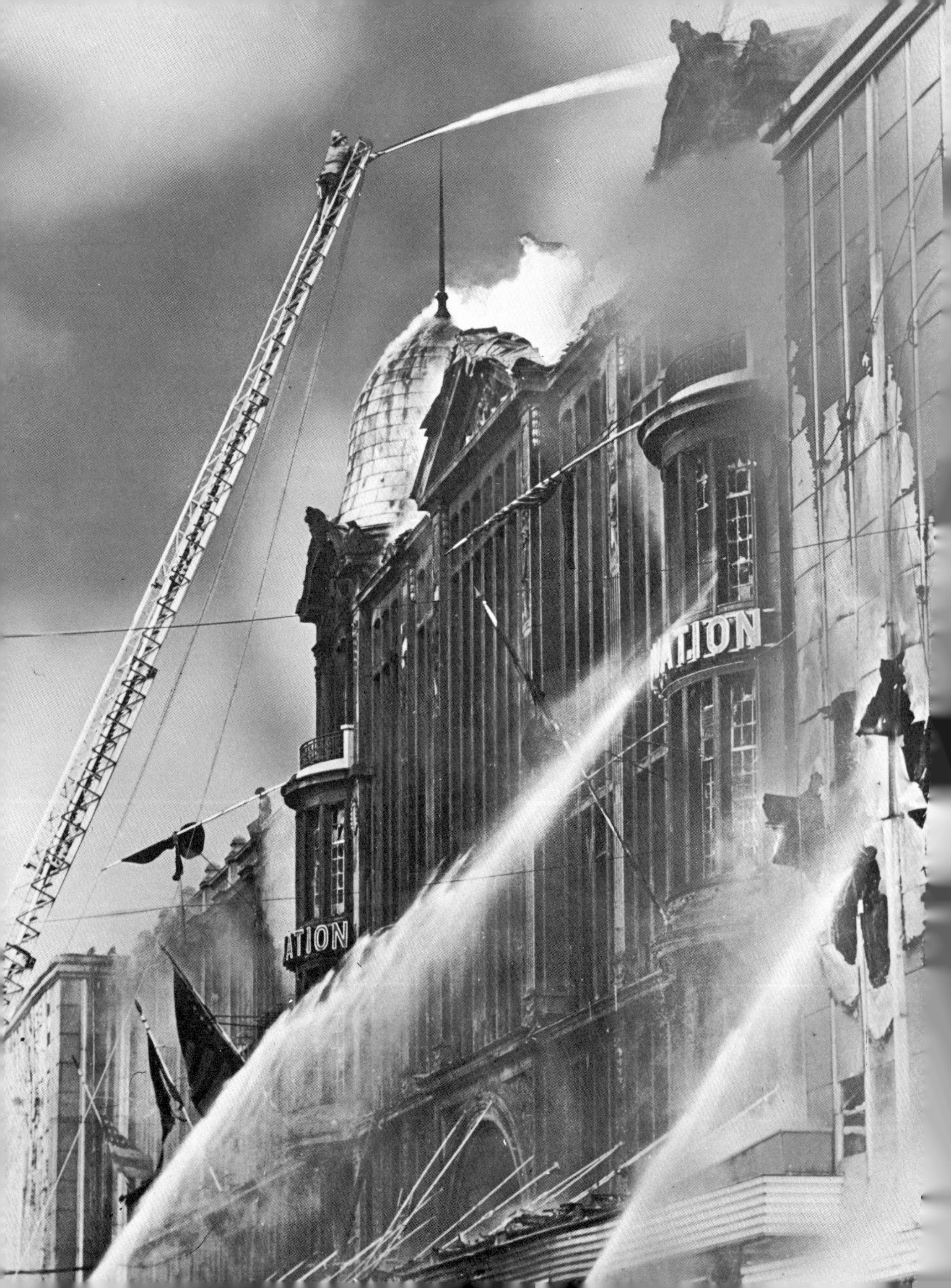
NATION
ATION

Firemen bring under control the blaze at L'Innovation department store in Brussels.

to use as an upholstery factory. Because the management were worried about thefts, they kept the fire escape door padlocked. The original key had been lost. The workers had decided to ask for a replacement key and had delegated one of their number to approach the management, though he had not done so.

In its whisky days, the factory's fire alarm system had been connected to the fire station, but it was no longer.

The workers realized that if a fire broke out they would have little chance of escape. On one occasion at least they had worked in the cold rather than risk putting on heaters. Their fears were justified. Just after 10 a.m. on 18 November 1968, fire started on an upstairs floor and soon spread throughout the three-storey building. Twenty-two people died. Helpless onlookers watched as screaming girls smashed windows and tried in vain to tear out the iron bars that blocked their escape.

The fire department later discovered that the fire escape was littered with rubbish, and that another access door to the factory had been nailed up. At a subsequent inquest, one of the firm's directors—another, responsible for the day-to-day management, died in the fire—said that he thought the workers should have been able to kick down the locked door. He added that the factory had a fire hose, although he did not know the source of water for it.

The jury, finding that the fire was due to the fault and negligence of the company, said that Parliament should consider banning bars on factory windows and extend reservations on smoking in factories.

The Taeyonkak fire: disaster as a spectator sport

It is a curious feature of this technological age that we have far better equipment and resources for recording a disaster than we do for rescuing those unfortunate enough to be involved in one.

Thus, on Christmas Day, 1971, in the South Korean capital of Seoul, press and television cameramen were quickly available to record the deaths of 162 people trapped in the burning Taeyonkak Hotel. They took dramatic photographs and film of people jumping to their deaths. But nothing, it seemed, could be done to save the victims.

It was the worst hotel fire there had been, surpassing the blaze at the Winecoff Hotel in Atlanta, Georgia, on 7 December 1946 when 119 died. It began on the second of the hotel's twenty-two floors, when a propane gas burner exploded in a coffee shop. The hotel was modern and luxurious, only two years old when it burned down and built at a cost of 2720 million won (£2,500,000, $6,500,000). Yet someone had skimped on safety precautions.

The hotel had no outside fire escapes. There was an internal staircase, but, once the fire had taken hold, this acted like a chimney, channelling the fierce blaze so that

In a vain attempt to save his life, a guest leaps from the burning Taeyonkak hotel clutching a mattress.

it quickly reached every floor. The exit lights in the hotel corridors were not equipped with batteries so that they would remain lit during a power failure. As a result, when the lighting went out, the guests ran from their rooms into dark corridors, not knowing which way to go.

Attempts to control the fire were little better organized, despite the arrival of some 1200 firemen, police, and soldiers. The fire engines were equipped with ladders that reached only to the eighth floor. A dozen military helicopters were used in an attempt to save people who escaped on to the roof. At least two people slipped from the ladders of the helicopters and fell 300 feet to their deaths.

Of the 296 people in the hotel when the fire began, 134 were saved. Those who could neither reach the roof nor the fire ladders, jumped. Some of them leapt clutching mattresses to break their falls. All those who jumped, and there were thirty-eight of them, died.

The fire blazed for eight hours, causing 830 million won (£885,500, $2,125,000) damage to the hotel. By the evening of Boxing Day, film of the tragedy had been seen on television in most countries of the world.

Monongah, Senghenydd, Gresford, Omuta: buried alive

There is a certain terrible similarity about mine disasters: the sudden explosion, the searing heat and flame, the choking poisonous gases, the roar of walls and roofs giving way, the fight for life, for breath, deep down in the underground dark.

Mining is a tough, dangerous occupation at the best of times. At the worst, it is marked by astonishing bravery and heart-rending tragedy. A mining disaster affects not only workers but entire communities. It is, thankfully, an area where the worst accidents are in the past rather than still to come.

Technological advance has cut the death toll. Safety standards have improved, sometimes not without opposition from mine owners. Hopefully, never again will 1572 miners die in a single catastrophe, as happened at the Honkeiko colliery in China, in 1942.

The disaster at the Monongah mine, West Virginia—the worst ever in the United States—happened on 6 December 1907. There were 500 miners underground, many of them Polish or Italian.

Few escaped the explosion, which destroyed the plant and buildings on the surface and blocked the main entrance to the workings. A couple survived, miraculously, by being blown up the ventilating shaft and somehow escaping serious injury.

Rescue work had to be abandoned when fire broke out below. It was difficult to discover exactly how many had died since there were a hundred workers, boys and mule drivers, of whom no record was kept. The figure was fixed, finally, at 361.

The worst mine accident in Britain happened at Senghenydd, Wales, on 14 October 1913. At 8.20 a.m., two hours after the day shift had started work, a violent explosion followed by fire killed 439 of the 940 miners who were underground at the time.

It was not the first disaster at the colliery.

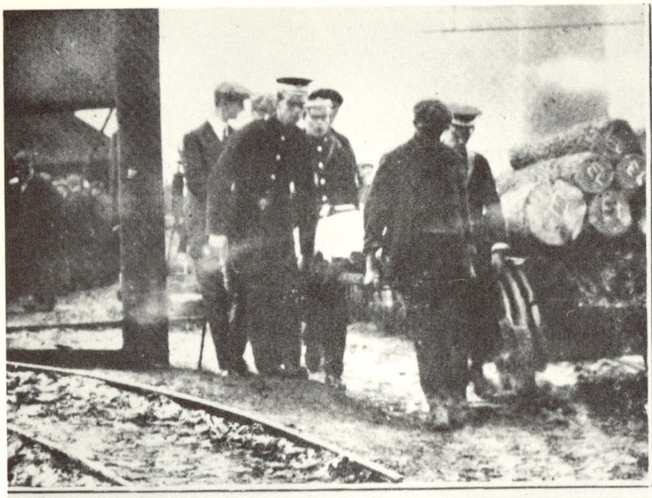

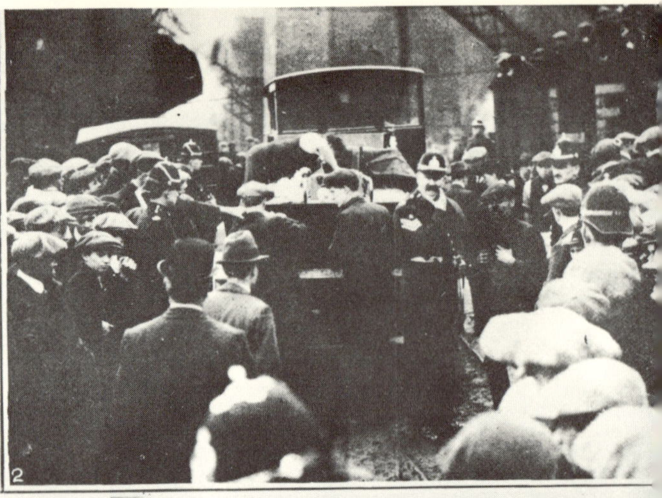
2

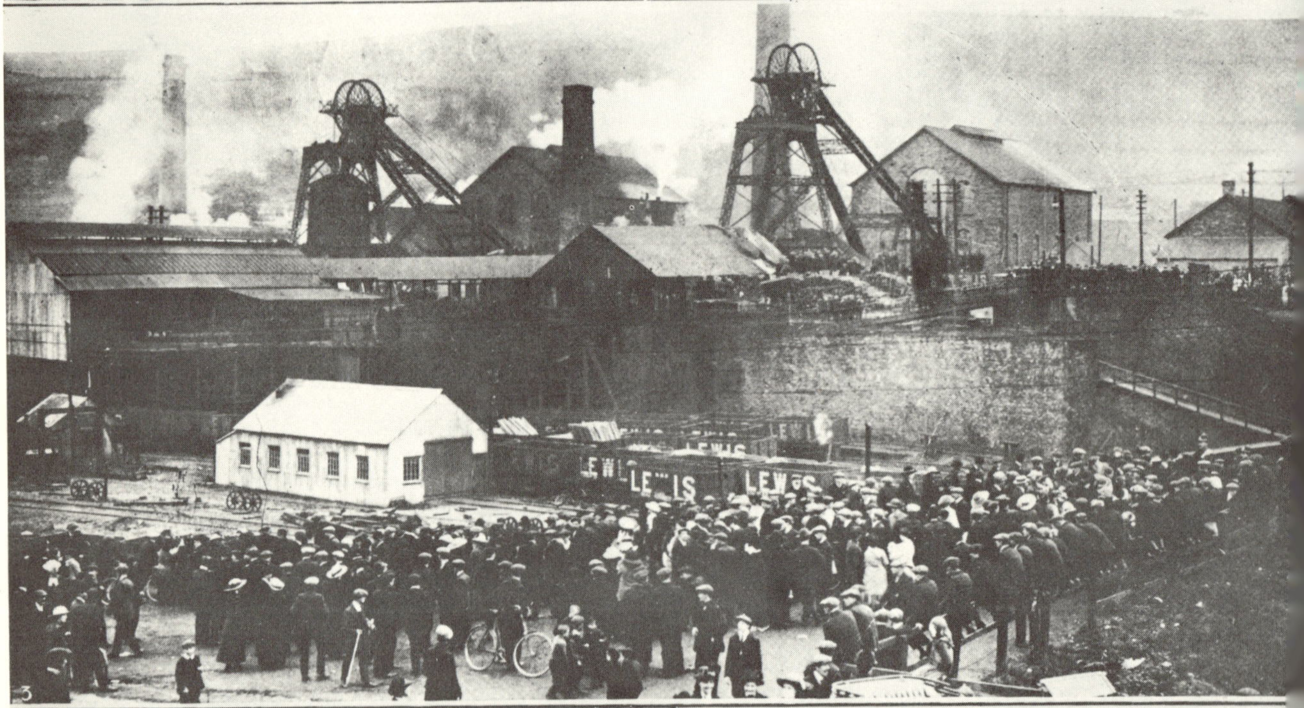

3

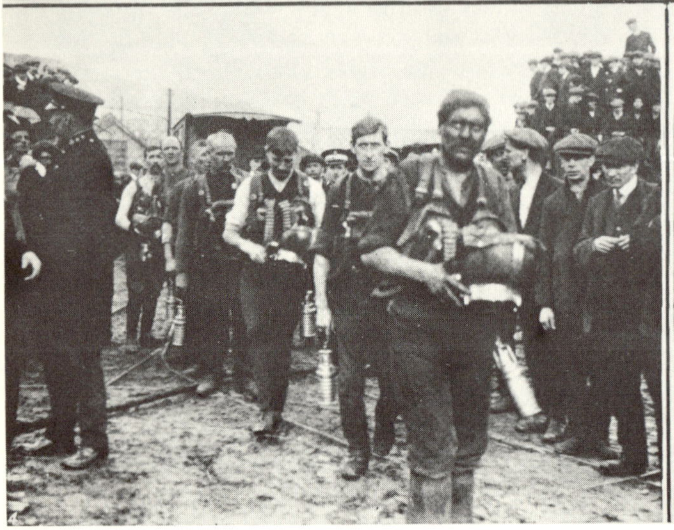
4

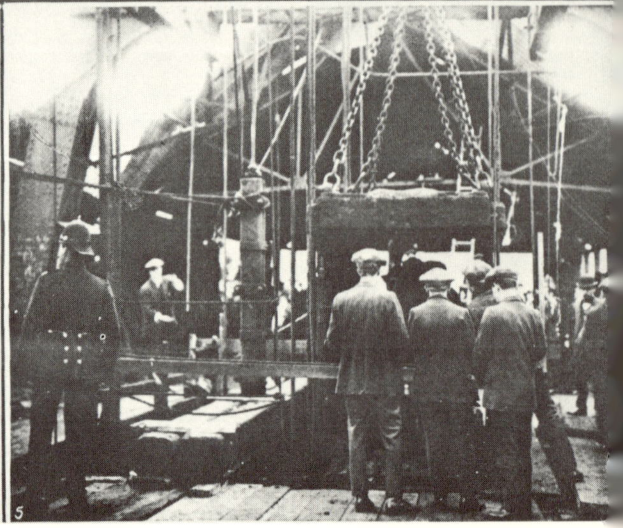
5

Scenes after the explosion at the Universal Colliery, Senghenydd. *Top left* dead bodies are brought to the surface. *Top right* an ambulance waits at the pit head. *Centre* the colliery after the disaster. *Bottom left and right* a rescue team prepares to go down the pit.

Scene outside the Gresford Colliery after the disaster.

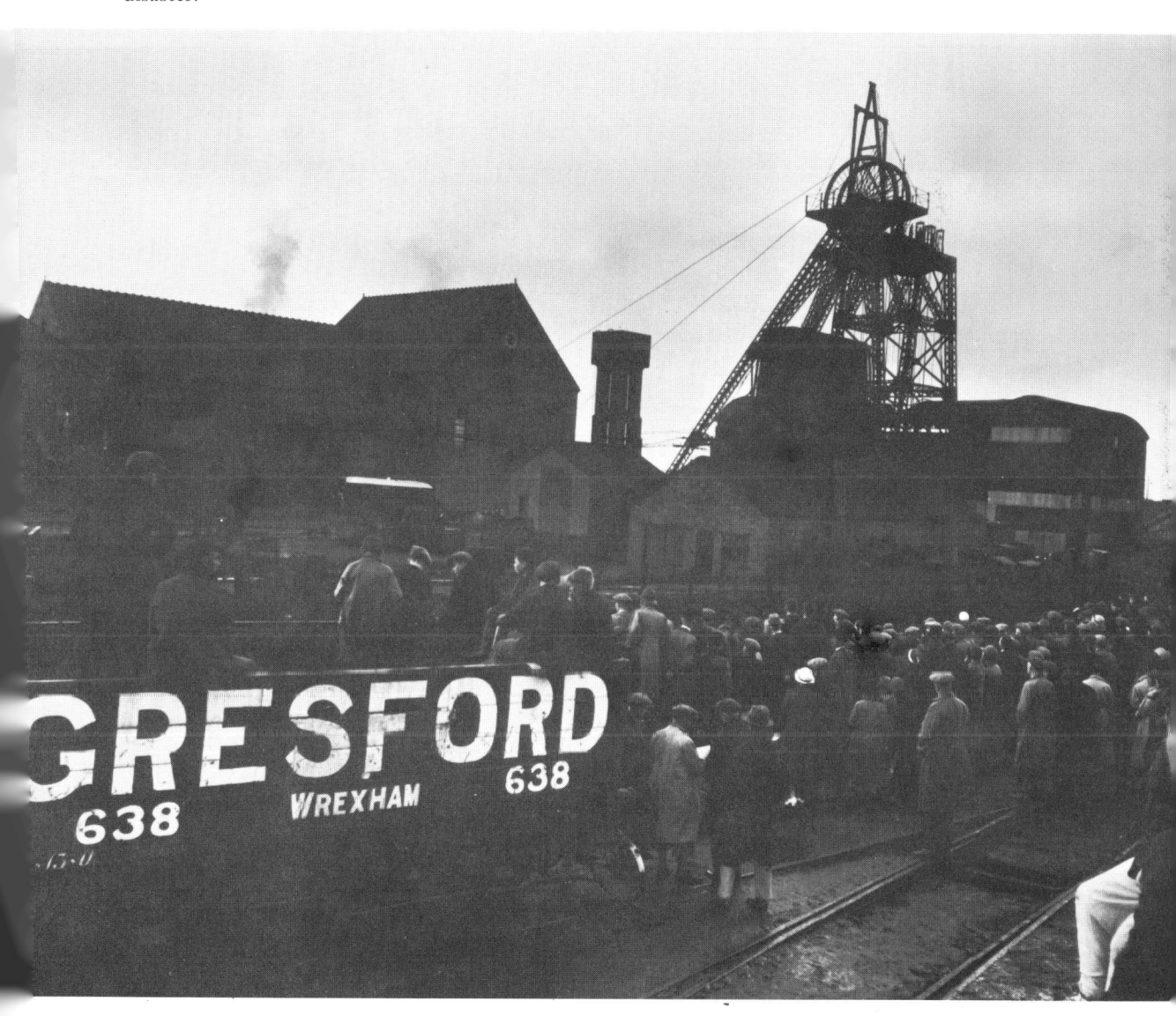

Rescue teams at work outside the wrecked entrance of the Monongah mine while, in the background, relatives of the emtombed miners wait patiently.

In 1901, eighty-one miners died, and one lived, in an explosion. Many of the miners who had missed that disaster died in 1913.

Rescue work went on under appalling conditions, for the fire was burning fiercely two days later. Teams returned exhausted to the surface with strange stories of a ghostly figure of a miner they could see in distant tunnels, beckoning to them.

In one short street in the mining village, there were twenty dead. One woman lost her husband, her four sons, and three brothers. But eighteen men were discovered alive sixteen hours after the explosion.

It was caused, an inquiry decided, probably by sparks from an electric signalling apparatus igniting gas which had been liberated by heavy falls of coal. The previous year, an explosion in a nearby mine had been caused by an electric bell sparking, and a letter of warning had been sent to other mine owners. The inquiry also criticized the inadequacy of the water supply for fighting the fire.

The previous worst British mine explosion had been at Hulton Colliery in Lancashire, on 21 December 1910, when 344 died.

There were more miners than usual working on the Friday night shift at Gresford Colliery, three miles from Wrexham, Wales, on 23 September 1934 because they liked to have Saturday free to watch a local football game.

About 400 were below when an explosion started a blaze so fierce that rescuers likened it to hell fire. It barred the way to the turning which led to the workings where the men were trapped, so that the rescue teams were helpless until the fire could be put out.

Two men died, overcome by fumes, trying to save their fellow workers. A day later, with 260 miners presumed dead and with the fire still raging, the pit was sealed because of the danger. It meant the loss of employment for more than 1800 workers.

Thirty hours later, a further series of explosions blew off the seal over the main shaft, killing a man. The final number of the dead was 264. It was not for seven months that miners were allowed to venture down the pit again.

On 1 November 1963 477 miners died in an accident at the Mikawa pit, Omuta, the worst mine disaster in Japan since 1914, when 687 workers had been killed in an explosion at Fukuoka.

6 Suffer the little children

The fire at Lake View School: no way out

There were 360 children, aged from six to fourteen, at their lessons in Lake View school, Collingwood, a suburb of Ohio, on the morning of 4 March 1908. In the basement of the building, a furnace overheated. Before long, the walls and ceiling of the basement began to smoulder and suddenly burst into flame.

The fire spread so swiftly that it took the pupils by surprise. The school was ill designed, with narrow corridors. There were two exits, but one was never used and kept shut so that there was only one way out of the blazing building.

Most of the children ran towards that exit. A few jumped from the windows and were badly injured. But most ran for the door in panic. The door opened inward. Those that reached it first had difficulty in opening it against the crush of children behind them.

The younger children were knocked to the ground in the scrimmage and there suffocated. Others were overcome by the smoke and fumes. Of the 360 children, only eighty escaped without injury. Nine teachers died, together with 171 of their pupils. The blaze was so fierce that the roof and the floors fell into the basement, leaving only the outside walls of the school standing.

General Slocum: corruption breeds corruption

It was a perfect day for a picnic, was 4 June 1904. A bright sun beat down out of a cloudless sky on to New York City, where 1800 mothers and children marched to the pier on East River, a blaring band heading the parade. The occasion was a Sunday School outing arranged by St Mark's Evangelical Lutheran Church, which obviously had a large and enthusiastic congregation.

The picnic site was Forest Grove at Long Island Sound. But, first, came a trip down river on the steamboat General Slocum. After an hour, fire broke out in the ship's storage room which contained oil, paint, and rope.

The alarm was sounded, but it made little difference. There was no water for the fire hoses, since the pumps did not work. The flames quickly spread, and the children began to scream and panic. The captain later claimed that he tried to run the blazing boat on to the nearest point of the shore, but that the engine room failed to respond to his signal.

As it was, the General Slocum steamed down river for a further half mile before it was beached. As it hit the shore, the hurricane deck collapsed on the terrified mothers and their children.

The crew behaved in a cowardly manner. They had made no attempt to lower any lifeboats or rafts before they saved themselves by jumping into the river. The only crew member who died was a steward, weighed down in the water by the coins in his pockets.

Mothers had flung their children overboard as the fire raged. Some had clutched lifebelts, which immediately sank on hitting the water for they contained waterlogged cork. By the end of the outing, the number of the dead totalled 1030.

The disaster revealed complacency and corruption among the city's steamboat inspectors, for they had approved the boat's obviously inadequate fire-fighting and life-saving equipment. After a federal commission held that three inspectors had been lax in carrying out their duties, which was something of an understatement, President Roosevelt had them sacked and ordered a thorough investigation of the inspectors who remained.

The Gillingham Park Fête demonstration: a house on fire

For more than twenty years the highlight of a two day fête at Gillingham, Kent, had been a demonstration of fire fighting. It brought crowds from the two neighbouring towns of Chatham and Rochester, although it was not a very serious show.

Some of the firemen would dress up as women or clowns and, with the enthusiastic help of local boys and much shouting and screaming, they were rescued by their colleagues from a house built of canvas and wood, which was then set alight.

There were always a great many boys, recruited from scout and cadet troops, anxious to take part in the fun. Their parents would ask local fire officers if their children could be allowed to take part. The demonstration on 11 July 1929 was no exception.

The house was a three-storey building. Nine boys, aged from ten to fourteen, climbed up the ladders inside to the top storey. With them were six firemen in fancy dress. One was dressed as a bride, for, to add to the drama, the occasion was meant to be a wedding party. The plan was that one of the men would light a smoke fire on the first floor of the house. While the people inside shouted for help, a maroon would be fired as a signal for two fire engines, parked nearby, to be driven to the rescue. The wedding guests would be brought down from the top floor by ropes and ladders.

When the last person had been rescued, the house was to be set alight. There were plenty of wood shavings and oil-soaked material piled inside to provide a spectacular climax as the firemen played their hoses on the blaze.

But the well-laid plans went wrong. Far too early, someone set fire to an oil barrel full of wood shavings which stood on the ground floor. In seconds the house was ablaze, bringing screams of real panic from those trapped on the top floor.

Only the waiting firemen realized what had happened. Spectators stood around cheering and clapping, thinking that the bodies they could see burning were dummies. The firemen had their hoses working within three minutes, but it was too late. When they tried to put ladders up to the windows, the rungs were burned before they could be used. Nine children and six adults died in the flames.

'It was clamoured for. The relatives

themselves asked that their boys should take part,' said the chief fire officer at the subsequent inquest. At first, he defended the demonstration as providing an excellent training for real fires, but, under questioning, he later admitted that the event was done to create a thrill.

The cause of the fire was explained by a sixteen-year-old boy who had been going to take part in the demonstration but had decided not to because he was wearing his best clothes. He said that he saw one of the firemen climb down a ladder from the first storey and light the barrel. As the flames took hold, the man seemed to realize his error for he climbed the ladder again and disappeared. It is probable that he went up to warn the others of the danger. It was a brave gesture, and one that cost him his life.

The Gillingham cadets: in step to the end

The accident that killed twenty-four young cadets as they marched along Dock Road, Gillingham, Kent, on the night of 4 December 1951 was terrible in its combination of an unlikely sequence of circumstances.

If only the cadets had been walking on the footpath. If only they had carried a light. If only the street lighting had not been inadequate. If only the bus driver who ran them down had been driving with his headlights on . . .

There were fifty-two Royal Marine cadets, aged between ten and twelve, marching along the road to the Royal Naval Barracks, Chatham, on their way to a boxing tournament. As if they were troops, they marched in the road. 'Troops never march on the footpath,' said the lieutenant in charge of them, in court later.

The pity of it was that they were not treated as if they were troops. The regulations for troops and naval parties marching at night lay down that they should carry a white light at the front of the column and a red light at the rear. But the cadets, really no more than a youth club with a uniform, carried no lights, for they were not bound by military orders.

The road, bounded by a high wall, was dimly lit. One street light, indeed, was not working at all. At 6 p.m., a bus turned into the road. Driving it was a man with a fine record, who was due the next day to receive an award for twenty-five years' safe driving. The route was a familiar one, and he drove with just his sidelights on.

Towards the barracks, the road dips. Most of the cadets were wearing their blue uniforms, dark enough to blend with the night. As the bus began its journey down the rise, the cadets, then only fifty yards short of their destination, stepped in a patch of darkness.

They heard the approaching bus and moved into the side of the road. It was only when the bus was almost upon them that they realized the danger. One boy pushed another on to the pavement and shouted so that most of those in the rear of the column managed to jump clear.

The bus ploughed into the middle of the column of children. To the driver, it felt as if he had run over some loose stones. It took him thirty yards to pull up. 'I suppose it was the bounce over the bodies and the blood getting on the tyres,' he explained in court, when he was convicted of dangerous driving, fined £20 ($52), and had his licence suspended for three years.

Royal Naval police guard the ropes and markings that show where twenty-four young cadets died in Dock Road, Gillingham. In the background, a bus begins its journey down the road.

The cause of the accident was inadequate street lighting, lack of proper safeguards for marching cadets, and the failure of the bus driver to use his headlights, decided the Committee for Road Safety. The committee also concluded that the Highway Code, which advises pedestrians to use the footpath, should not apply to cadets since it was traditional for uniformed groups to march in the roadway.

At the children's funeral, there was a posy of violets on each grave, carrying the inscription: 'In memory of the very gallant little lads who kept in step to the end.' The Bishop of Rochester preached a sermon, telling the parents that their children had not died in vain.

'They shall yet save numberless lives by their untimely passing,' he said. 'The anguish of this tragedy has awakened the conscience of the whole country to the social sin of the continual slaughter of innocents on our high roads.'

He added: 'This Chatham tragedy has moved the moral conscience of the nation as nothing else that I can remember, and some day people will point to your sons' memorial in Gillingham Cemetery as an historic monument marking the moment when England at last took road safety really seriously.'

Those words may, or may not, have brought some short-term consolation to the bereaved. But, with the passing of time, they have acquired a hollow ring, as the slaughter on the roads has continued to rise and the twenty-four young dead of Gillingham have become no more than another forgotten statistic.

Aberfan: the continuing tragedy

To one person walking through the Welsh village of Aberfan on the morning of 21 October 1966, the noise was like thunder. To another, it sounded like a low-flying jet or trams running down a slope. One of the masters at the village school, feeling the building shaken, thought a plane had crashed.

Another teacher heard an eerie noise, like a whirlwind. 'The room darkened,' he recalled. 'And I looked out of the window and saw coming over the embankment huge boulders and rocks, coming down literally on top of the classroom.'

It was all over very quickly. A slag heap, 800 feet high, on the outskirts of the village slipped forward sending a huge wave of slurry, liquid mud mixed with rocks, down into the village engulfing houses and the school, killing 116 children and thirty-one adults.

'Our strong and unanimous view is that the disaster could and should have been prevented,' reported the inquiry into the tragedy. 'There are no villains in this harrowing story. Decent men, led astray by foolishness or by ignorance or by both in combination are responsible for what happened at Aberfan.'

That the tip was dangerous had been known for years. Sporadic protests had been made to the authorities, but nothing had been done. In 1939, a tip five miles away had slipped across a road, leading to a memorandum detailing the dangers of tipping in that area. But the memorandum had been put away and forgotten.

Tip 7 had been begun on Easter Monday, 1961. Every working day, 200 tons of waste

Workers sort through the wreckage of Aberfan in search of survivors.

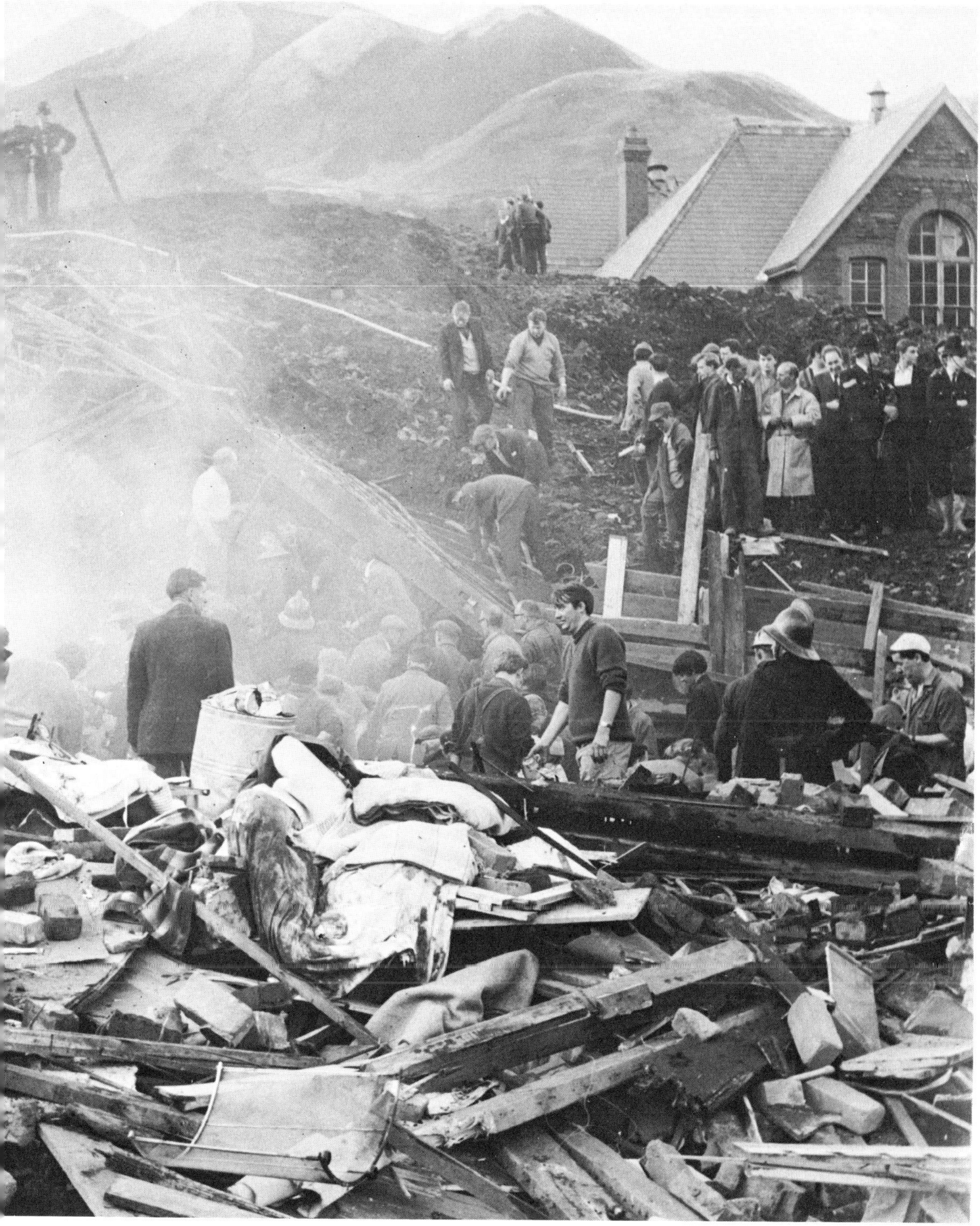

Aberfan, showing the path taken by the slipping slag heap as it engulfed houses and the village school.

were added to it. The telephone that linked the tip top with the colliery had not worked for two years, ever since someone had stolen the cable. Tip 7 was built over a spring.

Although the danger was apparent to many, their lack of action may have been due to the subconscious fear that protest would lead to the risk of the pit being closed down, and unemployment following. The Coal Board had no policy of controlling the siting of tips. The inquiry called it 'a terrifying tale of bungling ineptitude by many men charged with tasks for which they were totally unfitted'.

One of the lessons of Aberfan that still has not been heeded elsewhere in the world is that all tips should be regarded as potential dangers. They should all be treated as engineering structures and come under the same amount of control as is usual in other branches of civil engineering.

The aftermath of Aberfan was unpleasant. The tourists arrived in their hundreds, so that extra police had to be brought in to control them. The men who worked on the tip were treated as outcasts by the villagers, although the inquiry absolved them of any blame. As one of them said: 'All I was paid for was tipping muck and getting rid of it. I wasn't paid for anything else.'

The long-term effects of the disaster have been painful. Five years after, a psychiatrist reported that the prognosis for recovery was poor in eighty per cent of the adult cases referred to him. Some eighty-five children and seventy-three adults had sought treatment, only twelve of them for physical injury.

One boy had stopped growing for two years as a result of his traumatic experience. The villagers had remained understandably angry and hostile to outside help, and not all those who needed treatment had sought it. Local feelings of grief and terror were prolonged by the government's refusal to remove the remaining tips. It was not until July 1968 that the decision to leave the tips was reversed. It took two years to remove the six tips, which contained three million tons of coal waste. Grass now grows there.

But the psychological scars remain. Children suffered from lack of friends, unwillingness to go out, bed-wetting, and fear of the dark. Sleep brought nightmares for young and old. One child relapsed at the sound of heavy snow falling on the roof of his home.

Some adults are still taking anti-depressant or tranquilizing drugs and have failed to respond to therapy. The disaster upset so many families that some people could find no one to help them through their bereavement.

While most of the children will get over that tragic day in Aberfan, some of the parents will never recover.

Epilogue

Woodstock and Altamont—the future?

It was not until 1969 that someone realized the commercial possibilities of a disaster. For three years after, disasters were organized on a large scale, to the profit of few and the enjoyment of many. The occasions were called 'Pop Festivals'.

This, of course, is an exaggeration of the strange phenomenon, the three or four day concert that established itself after the success of the Woodstock Music and Art Fair, an Aquarian Exposition, three days of peace and music held on 15, 16, 17 August 1969 at White Lake in New York State. Such festivals lasted until national and state authorities brought in legislation to limit or even ban them.

Of course, the young flocked to listen to the music, which was often fine. But the events had much in common with disasters. Woodstock, after all, was declared a disaster area.

They were marked by death, inadequate supplies of food, little sanitation, primitive and sometimes appalling living conditions, with much litter and garbage, and air lifts to bring in supplies and carry out those in need of hospital treatment. After Woodstock, too, the occasions attracted tourists, people in search of a thrill, just as authentic disasters attract hordes of morbid sightseers.

If Woodstock had never happened, then there would have been no Altamont, a rock festival that ended a dream of innocence, that killed the belief that love and peace and music were enough to change the world. After Altamont, the alternative culture of the young became tougher and more violent.

Woodstock is important not for what it was, but for what it was made to seem, by that process of instant mythology that is part of the technique of mass merchandising.

> It was more than a pow-wow . . . it was a holy invocation . . . a summit meeting of the world that was to come.
>
> This time the earth was strangely consecrated by the boys and girls who came from all over the land to find what meaning life held and to find it with each other.

That is, in part, how the film of Woodstock, seen all over the world, was sold by Warner Brothers. There were other opinions about the festival. Michael Wadleigh, the young radical director who actually made the film, described it privately as 'a Nuremburg rally with music'.

It was Warner's hard sell that gave the event an undue prominence, as if the millenium had arrived. They were exploiting the wishful thinking that was one of the main weaknesses of the counter culture.

Rock music was the culture's main means of communication. They believed that rock was revolutionary in content and, for many, listening to it was a revolutionary act. They behaved as if singing about freedom was enough to achieve it.

This showed at Woodstock during Country Joe's performance of one of rock's most politically effective songs, *Fixin' To Die Rag*. 'Listen people,' he said. 'I don't know how you expect to ever stop the war (in Vietnam) if you can't sing any better than that.'

The belief that thinking could make it so showed as thunderclouds gathered over the festival site, Max Yasgur's 600-acre farm. Someone shouts: 'Hey, if you think really hard, maybe we can stop this rain,' and the crowd takes up a chant of 'No rain . . . No rain'. Of course, it poured. It rained, on and off, for fifteen hours, turning the ground into a mess of mud.

The same feeling characterized other festivals (of forty-eight planned in the year after Woodstock, only eighteen took place). But it was Altamont that exposed the insubstantiality of the dream.

Woodstock provided a paradisial myth for a generation, Altamont the counter-myth.

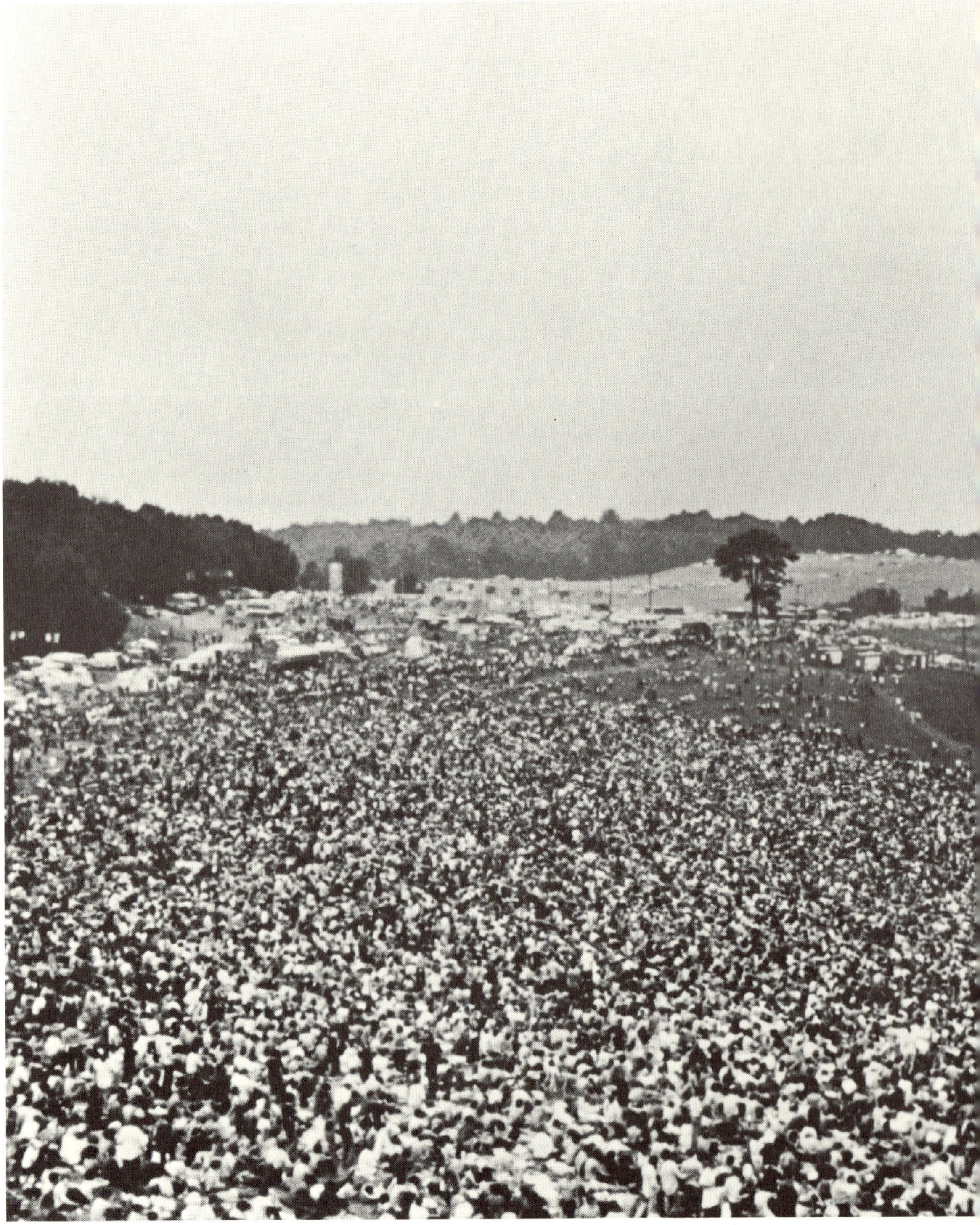

Both events acquired a significance far greater than the actual events justified. Indeed, more people died at peaceful Woodstock than at violent Altamont; but their deaths were accidental. At Altamont, amid scenes of squalor and greed, one person was killed with deliberation and brutality.

On 6 December 1969 at the Altamont Raceway, not far from San Francisco, before an audience of 300,000 the Hell's Angels, the notoriously violent self-styled outlaws and motor-bike enthusiasts, went on the rampage. As Mick Jagger and the Rolling Stones performed *Sympathy for the Devil*, one of the Angels stabbed to death an eighteen-year-old black youth.

The Hell's Angels' incorporation into the counter culture, despite the fact that they are violent and authoritarian, fascistic rather than commune-istic, can be blamed partly on two gurus of the underground, novelist Ken Kesey and poet Allen Ginsburg. It was on 7 August 1965 that Kesey introduced the Hell's Angels of San Francisco to the delights of LSD.

Allen Ginsburg was there and he even wrote a poem about it, which he read at the Festival of Two Worlds at Spoleto, Italy. There, he correctly defined the Angels as 'an American fascist group', but added that when Kesey gave them LSD, 'thereby there was a transformation'.

The belief that LSD was somehow sacramental, a truth drug that changed people for the better, derived from the proselytising of Dr Timothy Leary. For the Angels, LSD was merely another means of releasing their wildness and they mixed it with other drugs and their usual standby, alcohol. Nevertheless, since Kesey's introduction they had become tolerated by the counter culture and, despite their continuing violence, they even acted as a sort of police force for it.

In many ways, the young people at Woodstock were a product of that feeling of alienation within a generation that, in the 1910s and 1920s, produced the 'lost genera-

Crowd scene at Woodstock.

Altamont: still from *Gimme Shelter*.

tion' that found itself in Paris, and, later, the Beats, who combined a passionate protest with an insatiable wanderlust, as if it were better to travel, and travel anywhere, than to arrive. Ginsberg was of this generation, and Kesey's novels—*One Flew Over The Cuckoo's Nest* and *Sometimes A Great Notion*—were in its tradition.

What had changed was that the Woodstock Nation felt exiled within America. If they travelled, it was in search of enlightenment. Their image of an artist was not as a hard-drinking loner but as a gifted member of a community, high on drugs.

Kesey became a father-figure to an entire generation of the young who lived on the West Coast of America, introducing them to LSD through his 'acid tests'. He and his friends, calling themselves the Merry Pranksters, took trips in a bus painted in psychedelic colours. Significantly, the driver was Neil Cassady, now dead, who was the prototype for the hero of the best-known beat novel, Jack Kerouac's *On The Road*.

During his 'acid tests', Kesey is said to have given LSD to at least 10,000 people, including, of course, the Hell's Angels.

Among the Angels that he turned on was Sonny Barger, president of the Oakland Chapter. Barger was also at Altamont, for the Angels had been given $500 (£190) worth of free beer to act as a security force.

Altamont was a free festival, although its purpose was to make a profit by producing a film of the event. (The result, *Gimme Shelter*, with slow-motion footage of the stabbing has, indeed, fulfilled that end.) The Hell's Angels were in a swaggering, bullying mood. They arrived armed with sawn-off, loaded pool cues and beat people without provocation.

Sonny Barger, in a radio interview, later explained their actions. Some of their motorcycles had been kicked, he said, adding: 'Ain't nobody gonna get my bike. Anybody who tries that is gonna get got. And they got got.'

Despite the film record, the actual killing is a little obscure. The black youth drew a gun. He was stabbed. He ran and fell and was kicked and died. He had two deep stabs in his back and wounds on his forehead and neck.

The Hell's Angel who killed him pleaded that it was 'justifiable homicide' and was found not guilty of murder.

Since Altamont, there has been more violence involving Hell's Angels. In August 1971, three Angels were jailed and thirty-six others found guilty after a pitched battle at the Weeley Pop Festival in Britain. The next month, at Watsonville, California, a twenty-six-year-old man was stabbed to death and a dozen others injured after a fight involving Angels and some other youths.

Something soured in the counter culture after Altamont, and it has never regained the cohesiveness and peacefulness that was evident before. The outcome has been such incidents as the explosion at 18 West 11th Street, New York, which destroyed a town house and killed young members of the Weathermen, a group who believe in revolution through violence. Police described the house as 'a bomb factory'.

(It is worth noting that bombing is as American as pumpkin pie, and rarely the work of militant organizations. A bomb explodes in the United States on an average of once every two hours. Apart from the 5200 bombings a year, there are usually around 70,000 threats of bombings as well.)

The real disaster is that Altamont managed to discredit the positive achievement of Woodstock, however brittle that may have been, which was that society could undergo a major change peacefully and that it was the new generation who would bring about that change. A recent analysis of world trends, carried out at the Massachusetts Institute of Technology using a computer, predicted that, on current form, civilization would collapse within a hundred years. One of the conclusions was that a more stable system, without economic growth, is necessary for survival.

The Woodstock Nation believed in such a society, guided by what their champion, the Harvard lecturer Charles A. Reich, has called Consciousness III, togetherness and love. It is these qualities that are evident in a disaster area. Tolerance, a feeling of community, an acceptance of others, a willingness to share, are characteristics found in those who live in extreme conditions, whether it be the aftermath of a large-scale disaster or, say, London during the blitz.

When the world has become more crowded, when people have greater leisure and live in a society where they are no longer treated as consumers because there will be less to consume, then such events as pop festivals may be seen as having provided an essential training ground for that future.

A tribal and communal existence, a way of life that can comprehend and overcome catastrophic elements, such as was briefly visible at rock festivals, may be the destiny of us all. The world may have to accept what Wavy Gravy, otherwise Hugh Romney, of the Hog Farm Commune, said at Woodstock: 'There is always a little bit of heaven in a disaster area.'

Bibliography

In compiling my accounts of the disasters, I have consulted the many official records, including inquests, trials, reports of inquiries and Royal Commissions, as well as reports published in the following newspapers and magazines: the *Daily Express*, the *Daily Telegraph*, *The Ecologist*, the *Guardian*, the *International Herald Tribune*, *Nature*, the *New York Times*, the *Observer*, *Other Scenes*, *Ramparts*, *Red Cross World*, *Rolling Stone*, *Science*, the *Sunday Express*, the *Sunday Telegraph*, the *Sunday Times*, *The Times*.

Any reader wishing to discover more about particular aspects of disasters will find the following books as helpful as I did:

Barker, Ralph *Great Mysteries of the Air* Chatto and Windus, London, 1966; Macmillan, New York, 1967

Barlay, Stephen *Aircrash Detective* Hamish Hamilton, London, 1969
    Fire, an international report Hamish Hamilton, London, 1972

Bullock, Alan *Hitler: a study in tyranny* Odhams, London, 1964; Penguin, London, 1969

Carson, Rachel *Silent Spring* Hamish Hamilton, London, 1963; Houghton Mifflin, Boston, 1962

Cook, Bruce *The Beat Generation* Charles Scribner's Sons, New York, 1971

Fangio, Juan *My Twenty Years of Racing* Temple Press, London, 1961

Fisher, John (editor) *Eye-Witness* Cassell, London, 1960

Gallagher, Thomas *Fire at Sea, the story of the Morro Castle* Pan, London, 1962

Ghosh, K. C. *Famines in Bengal 1770–1943* Indian Associated Publishing Co., Calcutta, 1944

Graham, Frank Jr *Since Silent Spring* Hamish Hamilton, London, 1970; Houghton Mifflin, Boston, 1970

Grieve, Hilda *The Great Tide* Essex Record, Essex, 1957

Hamilton, J. A. B. *British Railway Accidents of the Twentieth Century* Allen and Unwin, London, 1967

Hoehling, A. A. and Mary *The Last Voyage of the Lusitania* Longman, London, 1957

Hopcraft, Arthur *Born to Hunger* Pan, London, 1968

Leasor, James *The Millionth Chance* Hamish Hamilton, London, 1957

Leighton Isabel (editor) *The Aspirin Age 1919–1941* Bodley Head, London, 1950; Penguin, London, 1968; Simon and Schuster, New York, 1968

Lord, Walter *A Night to Remember* Longman, London, 1956; Holt Rinehart and Winston, New York, 1955

Mooney, Michael M. *Hindenburg* Dodd, Mead and Company, New York, 1972

Padfield, Peter *The Titanic and the Californian* Hodder and Stoughton, London, 1965
    Ocean Liners of the Past: Olympic and Titanic Patrick Stephens, London, 1971
    Ocean Liners of the Past: Lusitania and Mauretania Patrick Stephens, London, 1971

Reich, Charles A. *The Greening of America* Allen Lane, The Penguin Press, London, 1971; Random House, New York, 1970

Rolt, L. T. C. *Red for Danger* David and Charles, Newton Abbot, Devon, 1970

...nd Armin Mase *Railway Accidents of Great Britain and Europe* David and ...ton Abbot, Devon, 1970

...n *Subsunk: the story of a submarine escape* Harrap, London, 1958

Shirer, William L. *The Rise and Fall of the Third Reich* Secker and Warburg, London, 1960; Simon and Schuster, New York, 1960

Stewart, Oliver *Danger in the Air* Routledge and Kegan Paul, London, 1970

Taylor, Gordon Rattray *The Doomsday Book* Thames and Hudson, London, 1970; World Publishing Co., New York, 1970

Thomas, Gordon and Max Morgan-Witts *Earthquake—the destruction of San Francisco* Souvenir Press, London, 1972

Thomas, John *Gretna: Britain's Worst Rail Disaster, 1915* David and Charles, Newton Abbot, Devon, 1969

Warren, C. E. T. and James Benson *The Admiralty Regrets* Harrap, London, 1958

Wolfe, Tom *The Electric Kool-Aid Acid Test* Weidenfeld and Nicolson, London, 1969; Farrar, Strauss and Giroux, New York, 1968

Wolfenstein, Martha *Disaster* Routledge and Kegan Paul, London, 1957

Index

Numbers in italics refer to pages including illustrations

Aberfan disaster 9, 95, 96, 140–143; *140–141, 142*
acts of God 7, 13, 18
Affray disaster 60
Agency of Science and Technology, Japan 27
aircrashes 7, 9, 62–79; *see also* named air disasters
Airship R.38 disaster 63; *62, 63*
Airship R.101 disaster 64–67; *65, 66–67*
Aldeburgh Festival Hall fire 9
Apollo fire 79–81; *80*
Araki, General 16
Ardey Roburite factory explosion 117; *114, 115*
Astor, John Jacob 45; *44*

Balvano train disaster 41
Barger, Sonny 149
Beckerton, Peter 21
Bengal Famine 1943 29; *28*
Bent, Geoff 74
Bethnal Green Underground disaster 8, 40
Bolton football ground 1945 104, 105, 106; *105*
bridge disasters 86–91; *see also* named bridge disasters
British Airline Pilots Association 79
Busby, Matt 74
Byrne, Roger 74

Cali, Columbia explosion 117
Cambridge, Godfrey 9
Carson, Rachel 32
Cassady, Neil 148
Chaffee, Lieutenant-Commander Roger 79
Charlton, Bobby 74
chemicals and drugs 7, 8
Churchill, Sir Winston 19–20, 49
City of Liverpool aircrash 71–73; *72*
Coblenz box girder bridge disaster 91
Coblenz footbridge disaster 86; *86*
Cocoanut Grove fire 110
Colman, Eddie 74
Coney Island fire 125; *125*
Crystal Palace fire 125, 127; *124*

dam disasters 91–96; *see also* named dam disasters
Danube bridge disaster 89
Dautrey, Director French State Railway 39

Derry, John 97
D.D.T. 8, 32–33; Lake Clear 33; man 33; ocean life 33
Disaster Prevention Centre, Tokyo 18
Dobrovolsky, Georgi 82, 84; *82*
Duke, Squadron Leader Neville 97

earthquakes 7, 8–9, 13–14; *see also* named earthquakes
East Bengal Cyclones 28
Eddystone lighthouse 8
Edwards, Duncan 74
Elliot Junction 37
Empress of Ireland 53; *52*
Ernst, Karl 121
explosions 114–119, 123; *see also* named explosions

Fangio, Juan 100, 101
Faroux Charles 101
Farnborough 1952 disaster 96–98; *97, 98*
fires 8, 9, 13, 16, 17, 18, 109–112, 120–121, 125–131; *see also* named fires
floods 8, 9, 18, 19, 20; *see also* named floods
Florence flood 9, 22–25; *23, 24–25*; art

151

treasures destroyed 25; Levane hydro-electric plant 22
Fontanet explosion 123

Garrett, Eileen 65
General Slocum, Steamboat fire 136–137
Gillingham cadets, road accident 138–139; *139*
Gillingham Park Fête fire 137–138
Ginsburg, Allen 147, 148
Glasgow factory fire 8, 127, 129
Goebbels 120
Goering 120, 121
Gresford mining disaster 134; *133*
Grissom, Colonel Virgil 79
Guggenheim, Bernard 45, 46

Halifax harbour explosion 114, 117
Harrow train crash 41–42; *42–43*
Hawthorn, Mike 100, 101
Hell's Angels 147, 149; *148*
heroism 7, 21, 48
Heyerdahl, Thor 29
Hindenburg disaster 69–71; *68–69, 70*
Hitler, Adolf 120, 121
Home for Working Boys, Silvertown 119
Honkeiko mining disaster 131
hubris 8, 45
Hulton colliery disaster 134

Ibrox football ground disaster 105–106; *104*
Ichikawa, Sergeant Yoshimi 78
Ikuta landslide 26–27; *26*
Indiana State Fair explosion 112
industrial disasters 7, 117, 118, 127
Iroquois Theatre fire 109–110; *108*

Juliana, Queen 19
jumbo jets, risk of 9, 78

Kerouac, Jack 148
Kesey, Ken 147, 148, 149
Knickerbocker Cinema 106–107; *107*

Lagny train crash 38–39
Lake View School fire 136
Lakonia 8, 56–58; *57*
Leary, Dr Timothy 147
Le Mans 1955 100–101; *100*
Levegh, Pierre 101
Lima football riot 101–103; *102, 103*
L'Innovation fire 127; *126, 128*
London, risk of flood 21, 22
Long Beach earthquake 16
Lorado dam disaster 8, 95–96; *95*
Lord, Captain Stanley 46, 48
Los Angeles earthquakes 13, 16; U.S. Veterans Hospital, Sylmar 16; Van Norman Dam 16
Lusitania 8, 49–52; *50, 51*

Macklin, Lance 100–101
Manchester United aircraft *see* Munich aircraft

Maracaibo aircraft 78
Maremara, liner 7
Mars, Lieutenant-Commander Alastair 59
Mattmark dam disaster 94
Meakin, George 36, 37
Mediterranean Sea, pollution of 8
Mikawa mining disaster 134
Milford Haven bridge disaster 89
mining disasters 7, 8, 131–134; *see also* named mining disasters
Modane train crash 8, 37–38
Monongah mining disaster 131
Mooney, Michael M. 71
Morrison, Herbert 69
Morro Castle disaster 8, 53, 55, 56; *54*
Moss, Stirling 100
Muller, Paul 32
Munich aircraft 74–75; *75*

New York World 63
North Sea Storm 1953 9, 18–21; *19, 20, 21*; Belgium 18, 19; Britain 18, 19, 20; Canvey Island 20, 21; Holland 18, 19; St Philipsland 18

Office of Emergency Preparedness, U.S. 9
Omuta mining disaster 134
Otto N. Miller, oil pollution from 29–30

passive morbidity 9
Patsayev, Vikler 82; *82*
patterns of disasters 8
Pegg, David 74
Pegg, Jackie 74
Pittsburg explosion 118, *118*
poisoning 7
pollution 8, 29, 30, 33
Pop festivals 145–149; Altamont 145, 147, 149; *148*; Weeley 149; Woodstock 145, 147, 149; *146–147*
Princess Victoria sea disaster 18

Quebec bridge disaster 87
Quintinshill train crash 8, 36; *35, 36*

Red Cross 9
Reich, Charles A. 149
Reichstag fire 120–121; *121, 122*
Richards, Tony 97
Richter Scale 16
road accidents 7, 138–139; *see also* named road accidents
Robertson, Morgan 45
Rogers, George 53, 55, 56
Romney, Hugh 149
Roosevelt, President 137
Roosevelt Racecourse 1971 102
Rostron, Captain Arthur 48
Royal Opera House, Berlin 110
Russell, Edith 8, 45, 46
Ryder, Captain 60

St Elmo's Fire 71
St Laurent du Pont fire 111–112; *111, 112*

San Francisco earthquakes 13–16, 17; *11, 12, 13, 14, 15*; Briores Dam 16; Great Fire 13; Hayward fault 16; San Andreas fault 13, 16
sea disasters 7, 44–61; *see also* named sea disasters
Senghenydd mining disaster 131
Shaw, George Bernard 16
Shirley Smith, Sir Hubert 91
Shizukuishi aircraft 78–79
Shute, Neville 65
Silver Bridge disaster 87, 88, 89; *88*
Silvertown explosion 119
Simon, Sir John 64
Smith, Captain E. J. 45, 46, 48; *44*
Soyuz II disaster 81–84; *82, 83, 84*
Spehl, Eric 71
Staten Island aircraft 77; *76–77*
Stead, W. T. 45
Strauss, Isadore 45; *44*

Taeyonkak Hotel fire 9, 129, 131; *130*
Tay bridge 37
Taylor, Tommy 74
Thetis disaster 8, 58, 59; *59*
Thomas, J. P. L. 60
Thompson, Air Minister Lord 64
Thresher, USS, disaster 61; *61*
Tinsley, James 36, 37
Tinsley Viaduct 91
Titanic 8, 9, 45–49; *44, 47*
Titanic Salvage Company 48–49
Togler, Ernst 121
Tokyo earthquakes 16–18; *17*; Asakusa Tower 16; Ueno Railway station 17
Torrey Canyon disaster 8, 29–32; *30, 31*; effect on British coast 30, 32; effect on French coast 32
train crashes 7, 8, 36–43; *see also* named train disasters

U.S. Geological Survey 96

Vaiont dam disaster 9, 91–94; *92–93, 94*
Van der Lubbe, Marinus 120; *121*
Venice flood 25–26; *22*
Victoria Hall, Sunderland 1883 8
Victoria, Queen 125
Violett, Dennis 74
Volkov, Vladislav 81, 82; *82*
von Hindenburg, President 86
Voss, Albert 71, 73

Wadleigh, Michael 145
warnings 9
Whelan, Billy 74
White, Lieutenant Colonel Edward 79
Wietfedt, Heinrich 46
Wilson, Harold 32
Winecoff Hotel fire 129
Woods, Lieutenant Frederick 8, 58
Woolley, Douglas 49

Yarra bridge disaster 89; *90*
Yevtushenko, Yévgeny 83
Yokohama earthquake 16, 17